To renew this book, phone 0845 1202811 or visit
our website at www.libcat.oxfordshire.gov.uk
You will need your library PIN number
(available from your library)

OXFORDSHIRE
COUNTY COUNCIL
SOCIAL & COMMUNITY SERVICES
www.oxfordshire.gov.uk

3302747458

FRANCIS FRITH'S

OXFORD PHOTOGRAPHIC MEMORIES

THE FRANCIS FRITH COLLECTION

www.francisfrith.com

PHOTOGRAPHIC MEMORIES

Francis Frith's
AROUND OXFORD

Nick Channer

First published in the United Kingdom in 2000 by
The Francis Frith Collection

Text and Design copyright © The Francis Frith Collection
Photographs copyright © The Francis Frith Collection

The Frith photographs and the Frith logo are reproduced under licence from Heritage
Photographic Resources Ltd, the owners of the Frith archive and trademarks

British Library Cataloguing in Publication Data

Around Oxford
Nick Channer
ISBN 1-85937-411-5

The Francis Frith Collection
Frith's Barn, Teffont,
Salisbury, Wiltshire SP3 5QP
Tel: +44 (0) 1722 716 376
Email: info@francisfrith.co.uk
www.francisfrith.com

Printed and bound in Great Britain

Front Cover: **OXFORD, 'THE EIGHTS' 1922** 72063t

The colour-tinting is for illustrative purposes only, and is not intended to be historically accurate

CONTENTS

FRANCIS FRITH: *Victorian Pioneer*

FRANCIS FRITH, Victorian founder of the world-famous photographic archive, was a complex and multitudinous man. A devout Quaker and a highly successful Victorian businessman, he was both philosophic by nature and pioneering in outlook.

By 1855 Francis Frith had already established a wholesale grocery business in Liverpool, and sold it for the astonishing sum of £200,000, which is the equivalent today of over £15,000,000. Now a multi-millionaire, he was able to indulge his passion for travel. As a child he had pored over travel books written by early explorers, and his fancy and imagination had been stirred by family holidays to the sublime mountain regions of Wales and Scotland. 'What a land of spirit-stirring and enriching scenes and places!' he had written. He was to return to these scenes of grandeur in later years to 'recapture the thousands of vivid and tender memories', but with a different purpose. Now in his thirties, and captivated by the new science of photography, Frith set out on a series of pioneering journeys to the Nile regions that occupied him from 1856 until 1860.

INTRIGUE AND ADVENTURE

He took with him on his travels a specially-designed wicker carriage that acted as both dark-room and sleeping chamber. These far-flung journeys were packed with intrigue and adventure. In his life story, written when he was sixty-three, Frith tells of being held captive by bandits, and of fighting 'an awful midnight battle to the very point of surrender with a deadly pack of hungry, wild dogs'. Sporting flowing Arab costume, Frith arrived at Akaba by camel seventy years before Lawrence, where he encountered 'desert princes and rival sheikhs, blazing with jewel-hilted swords'.

During these extraordinary adventures he was assiduously exploring the desert regions bordering the Nile and patiently recording the antiquities and peoples with his camera. He was the first photographer to venture beyond the sixth cataract. Africa was still the mysterious 'Dark Continent', and Stanley and Livingstone's historic meeting was a decade into the future. The conditions for picture taking confound belief. He laboured for hours in his wicker darkroom in the sweltering heat of the desert, while the volatile chemicals fizzed dangerously in their trays. Often he was forced to work in remote tombs and caves where conditions were cooler. Back in London he exhibited his photographs and was 'rapturously cheered' by members of the Royal Society. His reputation as a photographer was made overnight. An eminent modern historian has likened their impact on the population of the time to that on our own generation of the first photographs taken on the surface of the moon.

VENTURE OF A LIFE-TIME

Characteristically, Frith quickly spotted the opportunity to create a new business as a specialist publisher of photographs. He lived in an era of immense and sometimes violent change. For the poor in the early part of Victoria's reign work was a drudge and the hours long, and people had precious little free time to enjoy themselves.

Most had no transport other than a cart or gig at their disposal, and had not travelled far beyond the boundaries of their own town or village. However, by the 1870s, the railways had threaded their way across the country, and Bank Holidays and half-day Saturdays had been made obligatory by Act of Parliament. All of a sudden the ordinary working man and his family were able to enjoy days out and see a little more of the world.

With characteristic business acumen, Francis Frith foresaw that these new tourists would enjoy having souvenirs to commemorate their days out. In 1860 he married Mary Ann Rosling and set out with the intention of photographing every city, town and village in Britain. For the next thirty years he travelled the country by train and by pony and trap, producing fine photographs of seaside resorts and beauty spots that were keenly bought by millions of Victorians. These prints were painstakingly pasted into family albums and pored over during the dark nights of winter, rekindling precious memories of summer excursions.

THE RISE OF FRITH & CO

Frith's studio was soon supplying retail shops all over the country. To meet the demand he gathered about him a small team of photographers, and published the work of independent artist-photographers of the calibre of Roger Fenton and Francis Bedford. In order to gain some understanding of the scale of Frith's business one only has to look at the catalogue issued by Frith & Co in 1886: it runs to some 670

pages, listing not only many thousands of views of the British Isles but also many photographs of most European countries, and China, Japan, the USA and Canada – note the sample page shown above from the hand-written *Frith & Co* ledgers detailing pictures taken. By 1890 Frith had created the greatest specialist photographic publishing company in the world, with over 2,000 outlets – more than the combined number that Boots and WH Smith have today! The picture on the right shows the *Frith & Co* display board at Ingleton in the Yorkshire Dales. Beautifully constructed with mahogany frame and gilt inserts, it could display up to a dozen local scenes.

POSTCARD BONANZA

The ever-popular holiday postcard we know today took many years to develop. In 1870 the Post Office issued the first plain cards, with a pre-printed stamp on one face. In 1894 they allowed other publishers' cards to be sent through the mail with an attached adhesive halfpenny stamp. Demand grew rapidly, and in 1895 a new size of postcard was permitted called the court card, but

there was little room for illustration. In 1899, a year after Frith's death, a new card measuring 5.5 x 3.5 inches became the standard format, but it was not until 1902 that the divided back came into being, with address and message on one face and a full-size illustration on the other. *Frith & Co* were in the vanguard of postcard development, and Frith's sons Eustace and Cyril continued their father's monumental task, expanding the number of views offered to the public and recording more and more places in Britain, as the coasts and countryside were opened up to mass travel.

Francis Frith died in 1898 at his villa in Cannes, his great project still growing. The archive he created continued in business for another seventy years. By 1970 it contained over a third of a million pictures of 7,000 cities, towns and villages. The massive photographic record Frith has left to us stands as a living monument to a special and very remarkable man.

Frith's Archive: *A Unique Legacy*

FRANCIS FRITH'S legacy to us today is of immense significance and value, for the magnificent archive of evocative photographs he created provides a unique record of change in 7,000 cities, towns and villages throughout Britain over a century and more. Frith and his fellow studio photographers revisited locations many times down the years to update their views, compiling for us an enthralling and colourful pageant of British life and character.

We tend to think of Frith's sepia views of Britain as nostalgic, for most of us use them to conjure up memories of places in our own lives with which we have family associations. It often makes us forget that to Francis Frith they were records of daily life as it was actually being lived in the cities, towns and villages of his day. The Victorian age was one of great and often bewildering change for ordinary people, and though the pictures evoke an impression of slower times, life was as busy and hectic as it is today.

We are fortunate that Frith was a photographer of the people, dedicated to recording the minutiae of everyday life. For it is this sheer wealth of visual data, the painstaking chronicle of changes in dress, transport, street layouts, buildings, housing, engineering and landscape that captivates us so much today. His remarkable images offer us a powerful link with the past and with the lives of our ancestors.

TODAY'S TECHNOLOGY

Computers have now made it possible for Frith's many thousands of images to be accessed almost instantly. In the Frith archive today, each photograph is carefully 'digitised' then stored on a CD Rom. Frith archivists can locate a single photograph amongst thousands within seconds. Views can be catalogued and sorted under a variety of categories of place and content to the immediate benefit of researchers. Inexpensive reference prints can be created for them at the touch of a mouse button, and a wide range of books and other printed materials assembled and published for a wider, more general readership - in the next twelve months over a hundred Frith local history titles will be published!

See Frith at www. frithbook.com

The day-to-day workings of the archive are very different from how they were in Francis Frith's time: imagine the herculean task of sorting through eleven tons of glass negatives as Frith had to do to locate a particular sequence of pictures! Yet the archive still prides itself on maintaining the same high standards of excellence laid down by Francis Frith, including the painstaking cataloguing and indexing of every view.

It is curious to reflect on how the internet now allows researchers in America and elsewhere greater instant access to the archive than Frith himself ever enjoyed. Many thousands of individual views can be called up on screen within seconds on one of the Frith internet sites, enabling people living continents away to revisit the streets of their ancestral home town, or view places in Britain where they have enjoyed holidays. Many overseas researchers welcome the chance to view special theme selections, such as transport, sports, costume and ancient monuments.

We are certain that Francis Frith would have heartily approved of these modern developments, for he himself was always working at the very limits of Victorian photographic technology.

THE VALUE OF THE ARCHIVE TODAY

Because of the benefits brought by the computer, Frith's images are increasingly studied by social historians, by researchers into genealogy and ancestry, by architects, town planners, and by teachers and school-children involved in local history projects. In addition, the archive offers every one of us a unique opportunity to examine the places where we and our families have lived and worked down the years. Immensely successful in Frith's own era, the archive is now, a century and more on, entering a new phase of popularity.

THE PAST IN TUNE WITH THE FUTURE

Historians consider the Francis Frith Collection to be of prime national importance. It is the only archive of its kind remaining in private ownership and has been valued at a million pounds. However, this figure is now rapidly increasing as digital technology enables more and more people around the world to enjoy its benefits.

Francis Frith's archive is now housed in an historic timber barn in the beautiful village of Teffont in Wiltshire. Its founder would not recognize the archive office as it is today. In place of the many thousands of dusty boxes containing glass plate negatives and an all-pervading odour of photographic chemicals, there are now ranks of computer screens. He would be amazed to watch his images travelling round the world at unimaginable speeds through network and internet lines.

The archive's future is both bright and exciting. Francis Frith, with his unshakeable belief in making photographs available to the greatest number of people, would undoubtedly approve of what is being done today with his lifetime's work. His photographs, depicting our shared past, are now bringing pleasure and enlightenment to millions around the world a century and more after his death.

AROUND OXFORD – *An Introduction*

At the very heart of the county of Oxfordshire lies one of Britain's most beautiful cities. Likened by Thomas Hardy's Jude to 'the heavenly Jerusalem', Oxford's history, beauty and tradition are admired in every corner of the land. As a city it ranks in importance alongside Rome, Athens and Paris, and even when its scholars have left to make their mark on the world, they return again and again to embrace that curiously indefinable 'spirit of Oxford'. In order to see everything that this city has to offer, the visitor, too, would surely have to return again and again - and even when he thinks he has seen every landmark and photographed every tourist attraction, there is always something new and unexpected to stumble upon. A visit to Oxford, 'that sweet city with her dreaming spires', is certain to be a memorable experience.

From the top of Oxford's highest buildings you begin to realise that Oxford, like Florence, another of the world's most beautiful cities, lies at the bottom of a shallow bowl encircled by gentle, protective hills. But why bother with distant vistas when this noble city stretches out below you, its numerous riches waiting to be discovered, photographed and admired?

Oxford has a golden heart - a compact area of less than half a square mile in which the visitor will find a hugely varied assortment of ancient buildings, monuments and treasured landmarks which sit cheek by jowl with houses, shops and offices. In recent years millions of pounds have been spent on the city, restoring and cleaning the stonework of the colleges and university buildings, which had become grimy and black with the inevitable passage of time. Some were even in danger of disintegrating. The utmost care was taken in preserving them; today this great seat of learning, designed by distinguished architects such as Christopher Wren and Nicholas Hawksmoor, looks as good as it did when they helped to create it.

Originally known as Oxnaforda, Oxford was a settlement of some importance long before the University came into being. It began with the foundation of St Frideswide's nunnery in the 8th century. It is first mentioned by name in the Anglo-Saxon Chronicle of 912, which records that King Edward the Elder had made it a fortified frontier position in his defence of Wessex when it was feared that the Danes might attack from the north. The settlement grew, and after the Norman Conquest of 1066, King William appointed his comrade in arms, Robert d'Oilly, to be Oxford's governor. However, it was at the end of the 12th century, when Henry II prevented English clerks from attending the University of Paris, that scholars looked upon Oxford, by now one of the nine most important towns in England, as somewhere suitable to continue their studies. The first group may have been joined by others from Paris, as well as some from other parts of Britain.

Oxford University does not exist as such. Each college is virtually autonomous, with its own rules and administration. It is the world-famous landmarks that form the real core of the University - the Radcliffe Camera, the Sheldonian Theatre, the Divinity School and the Bodleian Library among them. A stroll through the heart of Oxford illustrates the contrast between the quiet dignity of the colleges and these older foundations and the noise and bustle of the city streets.

Oxford has grown and evolved as a place of learning and a sumptuous treasure-house of medieval architecture thanks to the benevolence and generosity of some of the most powerful and influential figures of the day. William Morris, otherwise known as Viscount Nuffield, Bishop John Fell and Joseph Williamson, Secretary of State, were among them. In 1249, William of Durham left 310 marks to help support masters of arts studying theology, and in 1280 the University used what money was left to found University College, which now occupies a site in High Street, or the High as it is better known.

Two other colleges were founded prior to University College. During the second half of the 13th century, John Balliol founded the college which bears his name in Broad Street, and around the same time Walter de Merton, bishop and statesman, founded Merton College, famous for its cobbled roadway. Worcester College also dates from the 13th century. The trend for founding new colleges continued throughout the 14th and 15th centuries. By this time there was growing conflict in Oxford between 'town and gown' as charters bestowed upon the city from successive monarchs conveyed privileges to the University, which aggravated the city merchants. It was not until 1525 that Oxford could boast its finest and perhaps most famous college, Christ Church. Its great hall and magnificent art collection are an important part of any visitor's itinerary. The college chapel is the Cathedral Church of the Oxford Diocese.

Oxford includes five women's colleges which date from the end of the 19th century, and among the most modern colleges are St Catherine's and Wolfson, both founded during the post-war years. There are also several postgraduate colleges.

A stroll through Oxford's streets also reveals much about the city's role in the English Civil War. Oxford was the Royalist headquarters as well as the seat of Charles I's parliament. It was in St Giles that the King drilled his men, while the nearby Martyrs' Memorial, designed by Sir Gilbert Scott, recalls the burning at the stake of the Protestant martyrs, Ridley, Latimer and Cranmer, during the 16th century.

Oxford's rivers are an intrinsic part of the city's beauty and character. Folly Bridge provides memorable views of the Thames below and glimpses of the city beyond.

The castelated Victorian house by the bridge survives as one of Oxford's best-known landmarks. The Thames and the Cherwell, pronounced 'Charwell', unite near here, with tree-shaded paths and sleepy backwaters offering delightful vistas across lush meadows to the honey-coloured stone of the college buildings. Christ Church Meadow is espe-

Rowing boats and punts are available for hire at Folly Bridge, and here, too, there are river cruises downstream.

During the 20th century Oxford, like many towns and cities across the country, witnessed sweeping changes. The age of the motor car had been ushered in, and in 1913 William Morris built his first motorised vehicle in a

cially popular with visitors and local residents; and nearby Port Meadow, renowned for its vast expanse of open grazing land, has not changed since William the Conqueror presented it to the burgesses of Oxford as a free common. These damp meadows with their lush pastures attracted West Saxon farmers, and by the 5th century they had started to ford the Thames at nearby Hinksey. The Oxford stretch of Britain's greatest river comes to life during Eights Week in May, one of the city's brightest and most colourful occasions.

workshop at Cowley. By the late 1930s the car industry had made an enormous impact on Oxford, with new housing estates built to accommodate the thousands of people who worked at the plant.

There have been many other changes over the years, but at the start of the 21st century, Oxford still retains its elegance and grace. It remains a place of infinite beauty, beloved of dons and scholars, tourists and city dwellers. Above all, Oxford is synonymous with man's cultural heritage.

COWLEY 1890 26803
More than one hundred years ago Cowley was nothing more than a large village, its intricate maze of rooftops stretching towards the horizon. Today, the motor industry dominates this sprawling suburb of the city, and much of Cowley has changed beyond recognition.

THE PLAIN 1922 71998
Located on the east side of Magdalen Bridge, The Plain signifies the boundary of the old city. Just out of sight, the River Cherwell flows under the easterly part of the High Street. Close by is Magdalen College, the first building of any size and importance you pass on entering the city by the old London road.

FROM MAGDALEN TOWER 1890 26802
This view of Oxford's dreaming spires remains as
impressive today as it was when this photograph was
taken during the last years of Queen Victoria's reign. In
the foreground is the city's famous High Street, often
described as one of the most beautiful streets in Europe.

MAGDALEN COLLEGE AND THE RIVER CHERWELL C1950 033110
The college buildings have changed little since they were built at the end of the fifteenth century. The New Buildings, which date back to 1733, blend harmoniously with the older parts of the college; the hall has an impressive Jacobean screen and there are some valuable manuscripts in the library.

MAGDALEN COLLEGE 1890 26819
On May morning a famous Oxford tradition is upheld when the dons and the Magdalen College choristers gather at the top of the Perpendicular bell tower to sing a Latin hymn. This charming picture is enhanced by a delightful view of the Cherwell.

MAGDALEN COLLEGE FROM THE BRIDGE 1938 88122

MAGDALEN COLLEGE
from the Bridge 1938

The tower, marking the eastern entrance to the High Street, dates back to 1492 and took seventeen years to complete. The delay was probably caused by lengthy financial problems. During the Civil War Royalist forces defended the bridge here by hurling rocks from the top of the tower at the Parliamentarians assembled below.

◆

MAGDALEN COLLEGE BRIDGE 1922

This charming picture captures the atmosphere of 1920s Oxford. Punting on the Cherwell near Magdalen Bridge has long been a traditional summer activity for undergraduates and visitors to the city, though sometimes a paddle is preferable to a punt-pole.

MAGDALEN COLLEGE BRIDGE 1922   72007

MAGDALEN COLLEGE FROM THE RIVER 1922 72005
Lying in the shadow of Magdalen Tower are the buildings of the University Botanic Garden, founded in 1621 by the Earl of Danby and established on the site of a 13th-century Jewish burial ground. More than 300 plants have been grown here for both teaching and research.

CHRIST CHURCH 1937 88112
At the beginning of the 15th century, the priory and church of St Frideswide were the main buildings on this site. It was in 1523 that Cardinal Wolsey, then the most powerful man in the country, decided to found a college at Oxford. Wolsey dissolved twenty-two monasteries to raise sufficient funds, sweeping away the priory and other buildings in the process.

CHRIST CHURCH, WEST FRONT 1922 72010
Cardinal Wolsey had very ambitious plans for Christ Church. He wanted it to be much more than simply one college among many within the city. The size of the quadrangle, the hall and the kitchen give more than a hint of what he planned, but Wolsey fell from power before work could be completed.

CHRIST CHURCH 1890 26813
Robert Peel, William Gladstone and W H Auden were among the college's more distinguished students, and when John Fell was dean here, one of his scholars based a famous Latin epigram on him following a reprimand.

CHRIST CHURCH 1922 72009
The Cathedral's official title is The Cathedral Church of Christ in Oxford. It has a unique place in the history of Oxford. Not only is it the smallest of all English cathedrals, but it is also the college chapel of Christ Church.

CHRIST CHURCH, TOM TOWER 1890 26815
Tom Tower is such an integral feature of Oxford that it is synonymous with the city's world-famous skyline. Oxford simply would not be Oxford without it. John Fell, one-time Dean of Christ Church, engaged Christopher Wren to crown the main gateway with Tom Tower, transferring the medieval bell known as Old Tom from the cathedral to the college.

PEMBROKE COLLEGE 1890   26882
The college was founded in 1624, and the front
quadrangle was built between 1624 and 1670.
William Morris, the renowned car manufacturer and
philanthropist, gave benefactions to various colleges,
including Pembroke.
Dr Johnson was an undergraduate here, and the
college is famous for its half-gallon teapot.

ST ALDATES c1950 033137

With international visitors and tourists thronging the streets, St Aldates is much busier today than it was when this photograph was taken. Christ Church, sometimes known as 'The House', can be seen on the right, with Wren's splendid creation, Tom Tower, rising above it.

ST ALDATES CHURCH 1890 26945

Originally a Saxon church, St Aldates was rebuilt in 1004. After the Dissolution of the Monasteries, it was acquired by the Crown before becoming part of Pembroke College. Its members worshipped here until the college built its own chapel in 1732.

BRASENOSE COLLEGE QUADRANGLE 1890   26885
Founded early in the 16th century, Brasenose College takes its name from an ancient brass door knocker which, some sources suggest, was brought back here in 1890 after it had been removed by rebellious students to another college, Brasenose Hall, at Stamford in Lincolnshire.

QUEEN'S COLLEGE, THE FRONT QUADRANGLE 1890   26924
Neat manicured lawns unfold beneath the Hall and Chapel of Queen's College, crowned by a small but distinctive domed tower. Beneath it is a carved pediment decorated with symbolic figures of Justice, Neptune and Plenty.

HIGH STREET 1900 45181
On the right is the facade of Queen's College,
a glorious Grecian building designed by Sir Christopher
Wren's pupil, Hawksmoor. The first stone was laid in
1710 to coincide with the birthday of Queen Anne.

HIGH STREET 1922 71992
Queen's College dominates this fascinating
photograph. Beneath the cupola above the central
gateway is a statue of Caroline, Queen of George II,
who donated £1,000 towards the completion of the
quadrangle. Note the lady cyclists in their fashionable
hats of the period.

HIGH STREET 1890 26912

Queen's College, named after Philippa, wife of Edward III, was originally founded to educate 'Poor Boys' from the north of England. However, one of those deprived scholars was the enterprising Joseph Williamson who later became Secretary of State. It was he who transformed Queen's into the college it is today.

HIGH STREET 1900 45182

St Mary the Virgin Church stands on the site of an 11th-century church which was once Oxford's most famous building. The present church includes a memorial to Dr John Radcliffe, one of the city's most distinguished sons. Note how quiet the street is compared with today's modern traffic.

HIGH STREET 1900   45183
Designed by Hawksmoor, the delicate spire of All Saints Church is a striking feature of the Oxford skyline. The church dates from the 18th century, replacing a Norman church which was destroyed when the spire fell on top of it. Today, All Saints is the library of Lincoln College.

HIGH STREET 1922 71989
Soaring above the High Street is the spire of St Mary the Virgin
Church, dating back to the 14th century. The even older tower
is 13th-century. This impressive photograph highlights the
contrast between Oxford's distinguished architectural styles and
the modern cars and fashions of the 1920s.

HIGH STREET 1937 88069

When walking the street's length from east to west, you can appreciate the sweeping curve which gradually reveals some of Oxford's most striking landmarks. The dignified charm and distinguished architecture of its buildings sum up the beauty of this city.

ORIEL COLLEGE 1912 64076

The college was founded in 1326 by Adam de Brome, Almoner to King Edward II, who was its first Provost. Sir Walter Raleigh and Cecil Rhodes are among the more famous men associated with Oriel. The college was famously linked with the Oxford Movement, and Keble, Froude, Pusey and Thomas Arnold all became elected fellows.

JESUS COLLEGE, THE QUADRANGLE 1902   48623

Jesus College has long been synonymous with Wales. It was founded by Queen Elizabeth I in 1571 at the request of Hugh ap Rice, who endowed it and provided scholarships for Welsh students; the college chapel and library date back to the 17th century.

LINCOLN COLLEGE 1906   53698

Founded in 1427 by the Bishop of Lincoln, Lincoln College has a chequered history. Financial difficulties prevented the college from being completed: at the time of the Bishop's death in 1431, only the gate tower and staircase had been finished. The college's future looked bleak. However, various benefactors eventually came to the rescue, enabling the work to be completed.

LINCOLN COLLEGE 1927   79692
The magnificent hall is the oldest among the Oxford
colleges, with its impressive 15th-century timbered roof
still intact. Small and intimate, the hall is especially
attractive when fellows and students dine by candlelight.

ST GILES' STREET 1890 26914
Partly visible on the left of this photograph is Oxford's
Taylor Institute, dedicated to the study of modern
languages at the University. Statues symbolising the
Romance languages of France, Italy, Germany and
Spain adorn the front of this splendid building, which
was founded with a bequest from an 18th-century
architect, Sir Robert Taylor.

ST GILES C1950 033112

It was here in St Giles that Charles I drilled his men during the Civil War. Over on the left, screened by trees, is one of Oxford's most famous hostelries, The Eagle and Child. J R R Tolkien, C S Lewis, Charles Williams and other dons met here every Tuesday morning between 1939 and 1962.

KEBLE COLLEGE 1890 26853

One of Oxford's most striking buildings, Keble is characterized by its red and blackish-blue brick, polychrome patterns, bands, chequers, trellises and buff stone. Its exuberant design dazzles the eye. The college, designed by William Butterfield, was established in 1870 as a memorial to John Keble, where young men of limited means could be taught under the influence of the Church of England.

ST JOHN'S COLLEGE 1900 45188

This turn-of-the-century photograph depicts the Canterbury Quadrangle, famous for its two loggias and two libraries. The quadrangle was almost entirely created by Archbishop Laud. St John's was founded in 1555 and is noted for its fine gardens.

BALLIOL COLLEGE 1890 26905

A clock peeps into view high above the quadrangle of Balliol College, one of Oxford's three oldest colleges. Former prime ministers Edward Heath and Harold Macmillan were students here, as were Matthew Arnold and Graham Greene. The college was founded by John de Balliol.

BALLIOL COLLEGE 1922 72017

'It is fitting that Balliol, the most progressive of our colleges, should have so large a proportion of its buildings modern', wrote Dr Wells in 1897. Up until the early 19th century, Balliol's reputation was flawed, and the college was dismissed as 'a dear, dim drinking college'. Open scholarships and clever tutors helped transform Balliol's image.

SHIP STREET AND EXETER COLLEGE CHAPEL 1922 72050

Exeter College was founded by one of Exeter's bishops in 1314, though most of the college buildings have been restored or rebuilt over the years. The Victorian chapel was designed by Sir Gilbert Scott, and includes various tapestries by Burne-Jones and William Morris. Note Ye Olde North Gate Teahouse on the corner.

ALL SOULS COLLEGE AND THE RADCLIFFE CAMERA 1890   26859
Founded in 1437 by Henry Chichele to commemorate Henry V and those who fell at Agincourt, All Souls is distinguished by some of the finest architecture in Oxford. The tower displaying the college arms was designed by Hawksmoor. The Radcliffe Camera is one of the reading rooms for the Bodleian Library, its dome an outstanding landmark on the city's skyline.

THE RADCLIFFE CAMERA 1937   88079
Designed by James Gibbs and completed in 1749, the Radcliffe Camera was paid for by a bequest from John Radcliffe, and originally housed a collection of books provided by him. The principal chamber under the dome is where undergraduates come regularly to read and study.

BROAD STREET 1897   40021
Broad Street is famous throughout Oxford for its
assortment of bookshops. Two of the city's most
notable colleges, Trinity and Balliol, line the left-hand
side of the street, while the striking facade of the
Clarendon Building can be seen at the far end. Note
the ornately designed street lamp in the centre.

BROAD STREET 1890 26942

OVER TO THE RIGHT IS THE UNMISTAKABLE FACADE OF THE SHELDONIAN THEATRE, DESIGNED BY CHRISTOPHER WREN AND OPENED IN 1669. BUILT FOR MEETINGS AND CONCERTS, THE THEATRE WAS NAMED AFTER GILBERT SHELDON, THE 17TH-CENTURY ARCHBISHOP OF CANTERBURY. TO THE LEFT OF IT IS THE CLARENDON BUILDING, FORMERLY THE HEADQUARTERS OF THE OXFORD UNIVERSITY PRESS.

THE SHELDONIAN THEATRE 1922 72026

Designed by Sir Christopher Wren, and planned like a Roman theatre, the Sheldonian was his first major work on this scale. Opened on 9 July 1669, the theatre was named after its benefactor, Archbishop Sheldon. University books were printed here in the 17th century.

NEW COLLEGE
The Entrance Gateway 1902

The college, founded in 1379 by William of Wykeham, lies in the shadow of the old city wall. The gatehouse was where the Warden monitored the activities of his students. New College has one of the oldest quadrangles in Oxford.

NEW COLLEGE 1890

Many of the original college buildings are in the Perpendicular style, and survive as a permanent reminder of Wykeham's design. The cloisters and the chapel, the latter restored by James Wyatt and Gilbert Scott, are particularly striking. The connection between the college and Winchester School is still maintained today.

NEW COLLEGE, THE ENTRANCE GATEWAY 1902   48626

NEW COLLEGE 1890   26889

BATH PLACE 1926
Away from the city streets and colleges, visitors can stumble upon Oxford's hidden corners and sleepy backwaters. Bath Place, off Holywell Street, is just such a place. Its Victorian, Georgian and timber-framed buildings give it a fascinating mix of architectural styles.

ST PETER'S IN THE EAST 1890
One of the city's lesser-known buildings, St Peter's in the East is a wonderful old church which lies hidden in the shadow of St Edmund Hall. The church, which includes a vaulted Norman crypt beneath the chancel, is close to New College Garden.

BATH PLACE 1926 79312

ST PETER'S IN THE EAST 1890 26946

HERTFORD COLLEGE 1906   53700

Dating back to 1284, Hertford College had fallen into decay by the middle of the 19th century, though its fortunes were later revived by Act of Parliament. The college was founded as Hart Hall, and stands on the site of several previous halls.

HERTFORD COLLEGE BRIDGE 1922   72025

Another of Oxford's much-loved landmarks is the Hertford College Bridge, or the Bridge of Sighs as it is otherwise known. This outstanding structure, which dates back to the beginning of the First World War and is a replica of its Venice namesake, connects the north and south quadrangles of Hertford College.

SOMERVILLE COLLEGE 1907 57393
NAMED AFTER MARY SOMERVILLE, A SCOTTISH MATHEMATICIAN, SOMERVILLE COLLEGE BOASTS TWO PRIME MINISTERS AMONG ITS GRADUATES - INDIRA GANDHI AND MARGARET THATCHER. VERA BRITTAIN AND THE WRITER DOROTHY L SAYERS WERE ALSO STUDENTS AT SOMERVILLE. MUCH OF THE COLLEGE IS HIDDEN FROM THE STREET.

SOMERVILLE COLLEGE 1907 57394
It was in 1878 that the Association for Promoting the Higher Education of Women proposed to found a hall in Oxford for women students. The hall opened the following year with 12 students - initially as Somerville Hall, then from 1886 as Somerville College.

WADHAM COLLEGE 1902 48628

Sir Christopher Wren attended Wadham College, and the clock in the quadrangle was designed by him. The college itself was planned by Nicholas Wadham, and it was completed four years after his death. The chapel and hall are particularly striking.

FROM CARFAX TOWER 1922 71988

At the centre of this impressive rooftop photograph of Oxford is the city's splendid Town Hall building, an architectural treasure both inside and out. Queen Street lies at the bottom of the picture and is named after Queen Charlotte, wife of George III.

FROM CARFAX TOWER 1922   71986

Breathtaking views of Oxford are captured in this photograph of the city taken from the top of Carfax Tower. Among the most prominent landmarks are the Radcliffe Camera and the spire of All Saints Church. Down below to the right are the premises of Wyatt and Sons, Drapers and Milliners, as advertised on the awning.

CARFAX TOWER 1922 71997
A policeman directs traffic in this city centre photograph. It is here at Carfax that four busy streets meet. Carfax Tower is where Charles II was proclaimed King in May 1660. The clock is famous for its quarter-boys, which strike every fifteen minutes.

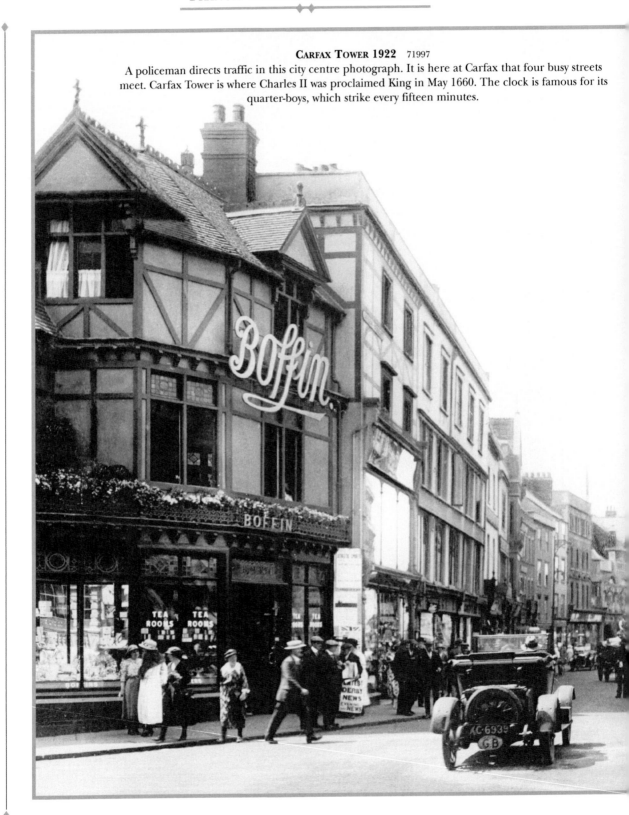

THE CARFAX 1937 88074

Over on the left there used to be a 'pennyless bench', where women sold butter and beggars scrounged a few shillings from passers-by. More than 300 years before this photograph was taken, the Carfax Conduit was built in the middle of the junction, conveying piped water from nearby Hinksey.

CORNMARKET STREET 1922 71994

The London, City & Midland Bank can be seen on the corner of busy Cornmarket and Carfax. Note the signs attached to the lamp standard, pointing to London and Gloucester. The awning of H Samuel, jeweller, is clearly visible on the right.

CORNMARKET STREET 1922   71995
St Michael's Church, where John Wesley preached from the 15th-century pulpit in 1726, is just visible further along the street. The Saxon tower is the oldest surviving building in Oxford. The Clarendon Hotel ceased trading many years ago.

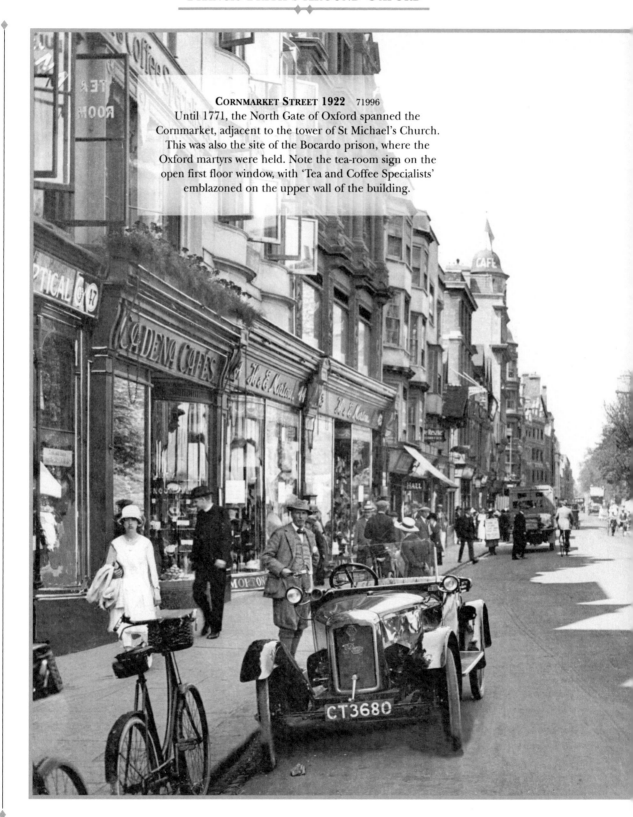

CORNMARKET STREET 1922 71996
Until 1771, the North Gate of Oxford spanned the
Cornmarket, adjacent to the tower of St Michael's Church.
This was also the site of the Bocardo prison, where the
Oxford martyrs were held. Note the tea-room sign on the
open first floor window, with 'Tea and Coffee Specialists'
emblazoned on the upper wall of the building.

CORNMARKET STREET c1950 O33129
The breathtaking outline of Tom Tower dominates St Aldates on the far side of Carfax. Morris Garages and the premises of Barclays Bank are on the right. Note that there are several cyclists in the picture; the number of bicycles in Oxford has grown dramatically in recent years.

QUEEN'S STREET c1950 O33124
Until it was demolished at the end of the 19th century, St Martin's Church stood on this site. The heavily-restored medieval church tower is all that is left of St Martin's, which was known as the city church; it was a focal point and meeting place in times of war or victory.

THE DIVINITY SCHOOL 1907
Built to provide a theological lecture room, the Divinity School dates back to 1427-80. The photograph depicts the school's magnificent vaulted roof, which consists of four arches and is beautifully decorated with figures and coats of arms. It was once used as a corn store before being renovated by Wren.

THE UNION CLUB 1890
Dating back to the Victorian and Edwardian eras, the Oxford Union consists of various buildings in the style of the Gothic Revival. William Morris, who, among others, painted the library frescoes, is said to have dined at Christ Church, his hair splattered with blue paint.

THE DIVINITY SCHOOL 1907   57372

THE UNION CLUB 1890   26943

THE CASTLE 1912 64171

At the centre of this photograph lies the Norman tower of Oxford Castle. Within its precincts lie a Saxon mound and a Norman crypt. The castle overlooks a branch of the river where it meanders between run-down buildings and small factories.

THE RIVER FROM FOLLY BRIDGE 1890 26948

This Victorian photograph was taken from Folly Bridge, which originally had a tower and gatehouse and was used by Roger Bacon, the 13th-century astronomer and scientist, as an observatory. In addition to Folly Bridge, Bacon also used the tower of Sunningwell Church near Abingdon.

THE UNIVERSITY BARGES 1890 26949

It is difficult to imagine Oxford without the Thames. It is this great river that helps to make the city what it is. The Romans called the Thames Thamesis, but where the Thames becomes the Isis and the Isis becomes the Thames again is not clear.

THE EIGHTS 1922 72059

The Thames is not sufficiently wide at Oxford for the conventional kind of race in which one boat, known as an eight, overtakes another. The broad, sweeping movements of the oars requires a lot of space. Instead, the crews begin the race in line before trying to outmanoeuvre the one in front by bumping it.

THE EIGHTS 1922 72063
One of the most colourful events on the Thames, Eights
Week takes place in May: it is then that the college barges
and the river banks rapidly fill up with riverside spectators
and those who simply enjoy the social aspect of the occasion.

THE EIGHTS 1906 53695
This photograph was taken from Folly Bridge; the reach from here to Iffley Lock is used by the college eights for training, and for the bump races known as Torpids and Eights. This stretch of the Thames is known as Isis; near here it meets its tributary, the River Cherwell.

THE EIGHTS 1922 72061

The object of Eights Week is for each crew to move up one place in a complex table of positions maintained from year to year. Each year every boat starts off in the position it occupied from the previous year in the table. The position of head of the river and the second, third and fourth places are the most coveted.

ON THE RIVER 1922 72056

This scenic stretch of the Thames, overlooked by Christ Church Meadow, has long been a rowing reach; at one time the bank would have been lined with eye-catching college barges, which were used as grandstands and clubhouses. Many of them have now gone - fallen into decay or converted into modest houseboats or holiday accommodation.

THE COLLEGE BARGES 1922 72051
During the 1920s, colourful college barges lined the north bank of the river as far as the eye could see. The barges were considered ideal for socialising and witnessing Eights Week in May. Today, smaller and more practical forms of river craft can be seen moored along the riverside.

ON THE CHERWELL 1912 64172

Hemmed in by a circle of hills and built on a gravel bank between the Thames Isis and the River Cherwell, Oxford creates the impression of sitting on an island. It was the damp climate here which probably drove the Romans away.

VIEW ON THE CHERWELL 1922 72066

A charming picture showing plenty of colourful punting activity on the Cherwell. The tree-shaded riverside path has long been a popular shortcut linking the Thames riverbank with the High Street and Magdalen Bridge.

VIEW ON THE CHERWELL 1906 53704
Like the Thames, the Cherwell has long been a popular river for boating, punting, fishing and bathing. Pronounced Charwell, the quiet, placid river forms the eastern boundary of the University Parks. A path runs along the east bank, reached by the high-arched Rainbow footbridge.

THE ROLLERS ON THE CHERWELL 1906 53705

Here on this tributary of the Thames visitors, locals and sightseers stroll undisturbed and yet remain in the shadow of the city. Wordsworth was greatly inspired by the classic view of Christ Church Meadow, beyond which are Oxford's magnificent spires and college buildings.

ADDISON'S WALK 1937 88125

The tree-shaded Magdalen Walks along the bank of the Cherwell are truly delightful and a perfect way to study the changing seasons. Addison's Walk is dedicated to the memory of Joseph Addison, who was a fellow of Magdalen College.

ON MARSTON FERRY 1912 64174

CUDDESDON, THE OLD MILL AND THE RIVER c1955 C292021
The 18th-century working water-mill lies on the River Thame, about a mile from the centre of the village of Cuddesdon. This photograph perfectly captures the peace and rural tranquillity of the scene. The Thame flows into the Thames at Dorchester, a few miles to the south.

CUDDESDON, HIGH STREET c1955 C292009
Cuddesdon was once the home of the Bishops of Oxford. There was a palace here, set ablaze in 1644 to prevent the Parliamentary troops in the Civil War from seizing it. A new palace was built by Bishop Fell in 1679. Bishop Bancroft, the founder of the original palace, is buried in the churchyard.

CUDDESDON
High Street c1955
This photograph shows Cuddesdon's long High Street, with the pub sign just visible at the far end. The village, on the eastern side of Garsington Hill, to the east of Oxford, boasts many stone-built houses and picturesque cottages.

CUDDESDON
Denton Hill c1955
Denton Hill is part of Cuddesdon. The name of the village is Saxon and means 'hill of Cuthwine.' From the churchyard there are wonderful views across the plain of Oxford to the Chilterns beyond.

CUDDESDON, HIGH STREET c1955   C292014

CUDDESDON, DENTON HILL c1955   C292006

CUDDESDON, CUDDESDON COLLEGE c1955 C292010
Cuddesdon Theological College was founded by Bishop Wilberforce and opened in June 1854. The college was designed by George Street, the distinguished Victorian architect; he was also responsible for the Law Courts, and the style is neo-Gothic with a Decorated chapel.

SANDFORD-ON-THAMES, THE LOCK c1955 S348012
The Thames divides into two here, with several weirs and a lock. There was once a Victorian mill here, though that has now been replaced by housing. Nearby is the site of a Knights Templar hospice founded in 1274.

SANDFORD-ON-THAMES, THE LOCK C1955 S348009
South of Iffley the Thames makes for Sandford. The lock here has the greatest fall of water on the river, with the water from adjacent Sandford Pool thundering over the weir, which is known as the Sandford Lasher. The Lasher has claimed several lives over the years.

SANDFORD-ON-THAMES, THE RIVER AND THE KINGS ARMS HOTEL C1955 S348004
The Kings Arms is 15th-century; much of the building was once part of a thriving paper-mill. This photograph recalls the days when the mill was still in use, and the chimney was something of a local landmark. A ferry service operated from here as early as the 13th century.

SANDFORD-ON-THAMES, ST ANDREW'S CHURCH C1955 S348003

Not much remains of the Early Norman church founded here at the end of the 11th century. Note the church porch, which was restored by Dame Eliza Isham in 1652 and bears the inscription: 'Thanks to thy charitie religious dame, which found me old and made me new againe.'

SANDFORD-ON-THAMES, THE MAIN ROAD C1955 S348011

The village is situated on a loop of the Thames between Oxford and Abingdon. Today, Sandford is a rapidly-expanding riverside village, but in the 1950s, it was a quiet rural community. Note the old RAC logo on the left.

WYTHAM, THE VILLAGE c1965 W259301

Pronounced 'white'em', this is one of Oxfordshire's prettiest villages. Plenty of stone-built houses and cottages stand in the shadow of Wytham Great Wood, and just to the south lies 700-acre Wytham Park. The house is now part of Oxford University. Note the White Hart pub sign on the corner.

WYTHAM, THE CHURCH c1965 W259302

The original church dates back to about 1480; it is thought to have been built by the monks of Abingdon Abbey. It was completely rebuilt in 1811 with various materials from Cumnor Place, which was destroyed by the third Earl of Abingdon.

Index

FRITH PRODUCTS & SERVICES

Francis Frith would doubtless be pleased to know that the pioneering publishing venture he started in 1860 still continues today. Over a hundred and forty years later, The Francis Frith Collection continues in the same innovative tradition and is now one of the foremost publishers of vintage photographs in the world. Some of the current activities include:

INTERIOR DECORATION

Today Frith's photographs can be seen framed and as giant wall murals in thousands of pubs, restaurants, hotels, banks, retail stores and other public buildings throughout the country. In every case they enhance the unique local atmosphere of the places they depict and provide reminders of gentler days in an increasingly busy and frenetic world.

PRODUCT PROMOTIONS

Frith products are used by many major companies to promote the sales of their own products or to reinforce their own history and heritage. Frith promotions have been used by Hovis bread, Courage beers, Scots Porage Oats, Colman's mustard, Cadbury's foods, Mellow Birds coffee, Dunhill pipe tobacco, Guinness, and Bulmer's Cider.

GENEALOGY AND FAMILY HISTORY

As the interest in family history and roots grows world-wide, more and more people are turning to Frith's photographs of Great Britain for images of the towns, villages and streets where their ancestors lived; and, of course, photographs of the churches and chapels where their ancestors were christened, married and buried are an essential part of every genealogy tree and family album.

FRITH PRODUCTS

All Frith photographs are available Framed or just as Mounted Prints and Posters (size 23 x 16 inches). These may be ordered from the address below. Other products available are - Address Books, Calendars, Jigsaws, Canvas Prints, Postcards and local and prestige books.

THE INTERNET

Already ninety thousand Frith photographs can be viewed and purchased on the internet through the Frith websites and a myriad of partner sites.

For more detailed information on Frith products, look at this site:
www.francisfrith.com

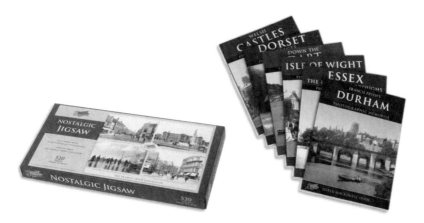

See the complete list of Frith Books at: www.francisfrith.com
This web site is regularly updated with the latest list of publications from The Francis Frith Collection. If you wish to buy books relating to another part of the country that your local bookshop does not stock, you may purchase on-line.

For further information, trade, or author enquiries please contact us at the address below:
The Francis Frith Collection, Unit 6, Oakley Business Park, Wylye Road, Dinton, Wiltshire SP3 5EU.
Tel: +44 (0)1722 716 376 Fax: +44 (0)1722 716 881 Email: sales@francisfrith.co.uk

---

See Frith products on the internet at www.francisfrith.com

FREE PRINT OF YOUR CHOICE

Mounted Print
Overall size 14 x 11 inches (355 x 280mm)

Choose any Frith photograph in this book.
Simply complete the Voucher opposite and
return it with your remittance for £3.50 (to cover
postage and handling) and we will print the
photograph of your choice in SEPIA (size 11 x 8
inches) and supply it in a cream mount with a
burgundy rule line (overall size 14 x 11 inches).
**Please note: aerial photographs and
photographs with a reference number
starting with a "Z" are not Frith photographs
and cannot be supplied under this offer.
Offer valid for delivery to one UK address only.**

PLUS: **Order additional Mounted Prints
at HALF PRICE - £9.50 each** (normally £19.00)
If you would like to order more Frith prints from
this book, possibly as gifts for friends and family,
you can buy them at half price (with no
additional postage and handling costs).

PLUS: **Have your Mounted Prints framed**
For an extra £18.00 per print you can have your
mounted print(s) framed in an elegant polished
wood and gilt moulding, overall size
16 x 13 inches (no additional postage and
handling required).

IMPORTANT!

**These special prices are only available if you use
this form to order. You must use the ORIGINAL
VOUCHER on this page (no copies permitted). We
can only despatch to one UK address. This offer
cannot be combined with any other offer.**

Send completed Voucher form to:
**The Francis Frith Collection, Unit 6,
Oakley Business Park, Wylye Road,
Dinton, Wiltshire SP3 5EU**

CHOOSE A PHOTOGRAPH FROM THIS BOOK

Voucher for **FREE** and Reduced Price Frith Prints

*Please do not photocopy this voucher. Only the original is valid,
so please fill it in, cut it out and return it to us with your order.*

Picture ref no	Page no	Qty	Mounted @ £9.50	Framed + £18.00	Total Cost £
		1	Free of charge*	£	£
			£9.50	£	£
			£9.50	£	£
			£9.50	£	£
			£9.50	£	£
			£9.50	£	£
Please allow 28 days for delivery. Offer available to one UK address only			* Post & handling		£3.80
			Total Order Cost		£

Title of this book . . . .

I enclose a cheque/postal order for £ . . . .
made payable to 'The Francis Frith Collection'

OR please debit my Mastercard / Visa / Maestro card,
details below

Card Number:

Issue No (Maestro only):   Valid from (Maestro):

Card Security Number: Expires:

Signature:

Name Mr/Mrs/Ms . . . .
Address . . . .
. . . .
. . . .
. . . . Postcode . . . .
Daytime Tel No . . . .
Email . . . .

Valid to 31/12/12

Can you help us with information about any of the Frith photographs in this book?

We are gradually compiling an historical record for each of the photographs in the Frith archive. It is always fascinating to find out the names of the people shown in the pictures, as well as insights into the shops, buildings and other features depicted.

If you recognize anyone in the photographs in this book, or if you have information not already included in the author's caption, do let us know. We would love to hear from you, and will try to publish it in future books or articles.

An Invitation from The Francis Frith Collection to Share Your Memories

The 'Share Your Memories' feature of our website allows members of the public to add personal memories relating to the places featured in our photographs, or comment on others already added. Seeing a place from your past can rekindle forgotten or long held memories. Why not visit the website, find photographs of places you know well and add YOUR story for others to read and enjoy? We would love to hear from you!

www.francisfrith.com/memories

Our production team

Frith books are produced by a small dedicated team at offices near Salisbury. Most have worked with the Frith Collection for many years. All have in common one quality: they have a passion for the Frith Collection.

Frith Books and Gifts

We have a wide range of books and gifts available on our website utilising our photographic archive, many of which can be individually personalised.

www.francisfrith.com

Flooded Yorkshire 2007
the pictures that told the story

YORKSHIRE POST

Flooded Yorkshire 2007

the pictures that told the story

at heart publications

First published in 2007 by:
At Heart Ltd, 32 Stamford Street,
Altrincham, Cheshire, WA14 1EY

In conjunction with
Yorkshire Post Newspapers Ltd
PO Box 168, Wellington Street,
Leeds, LS1 1RF

© The Yorkshire Post

Printed by Bell & Bain, Scotland.

ISBN: 978-1-84547-180-4

Fire fighters pass an abandoned car on Cliffe Road off Doncaster Road, Darfield Bridge. *Picture Bruce Rollinson*

CONTENTS

INTRODUCTION

AT FIRST IT had seemed like just another rainy summer's day – until age-old services ground to a halt and whole populations found themselves trapped in rising water.

Sheffield was virtually marooned. More than 100 people were airlifted to safety by search and rescue helicopters. Offices, factories and homes were swamped, leaving workers and residents trapped or stranded. Even the city's monument to its own Renaissance – the Meadowhall Shopping Centre – was flooded.

And two in Sheffield died.

A third life was lost in Hull, where the devastation was particularly severe and the community would later complain of inadequate Government response, and that it had become the Forgotten City of one of Britain's worst peacetime disasters.

It was not just big communities such as Doncaster and Rotherham which were hit. Pickering also paid a heavy price for the decision to shelve its flood defences when the beck burst its banks – pushing up the number of homes affected in North Yorkshire to 400.

Nearly 40,000 people in the region became homeless – including an estimated 30,000 in Hull, 3,000 in the East Riding, 1,000 in Rotherham, and 1,200 in Barnsley.

Some victims lost everything, having fled in the clothes they stood up in.

Businesses had to assess their losses, and in some cases these may have been so great that recovery was impossible.

There was, then, good reason to be grateful that something called "Yorkshire grit" – the stoic, phlegmatic spirit which defines the Yorkshire character – came to the fore.

It is evident in many of these pictures, so while they record great suffering and great destruction of property, they also celebrate an indomitable spirit.

YORKSHIRE POST

SPECIAL PUBLICATION SATURDAY JULY 7 2007

THE GREAT FLOOD

Scene of devastation: This aerial view of the village of Catcliffe, near Sheffield , serves a stark reminder of the day the rains came to Yorkshire and the suffering the water brought with it for thousands of people from our region. Today, the *Yorkshire Post* launches a campaign designed to get the help those people affected so desperately need. It is time for the Government to take action.

Pay us the money now

ALMOST two weeks after large areas of Yorkshire were first swamped by floods, tens of thousands of people are trapped in a living hell.

Properties are submerged under several feet of water. Sewage and sludge fills streets. Families are homeless.

It will be six months – or even longer in extreme cases – before a semblance of normality returns.

As water levels subside, leaving behind a sickening stench, the scale of the devastation becomes visible – and it is truly daunting.

In Yorkshire alone, the final repair bill could be as high as £2bn and exceed the financial losses incurred during the 2001 foot-and-mouth epidemic.

However, the national response to this crisis has, thus far, comprised two heartfelt visits by Prince Charles, vague promises of cash support from Prime Minister Gordon Brown and fleeting tours of the region by senior politicians who were effectively shamed into visiting the region by cries for help from flooding

victims that were, frankly, ignored for far too long.

It is not good enough.

Today, the *Yorkshire Post* challenges Mr Brown, who will belatedly tour flood-hit communities this weekend, to do three specific things without delay.

● Pay the full clean-up costs incurred by local authorities.

● Fund repairs to damaged infrastructure, like schools and roads.

● Ensure the money is handed over to councils within weeks, not months.

Mr Brown will also see for himself the need for his government to devise a coherent strategy to protect communities from the spectre of future floods.

While the level of rain has been unprecedented in Yorkshire, the abiding failure of successive governments to stop homes and offices from being built in flood-risk areas, improve drainage systems and build adequate flood defences contributed to the catastrophe.

Mr Brown now has a moral and political obligation to act rather than leave cash-

YORKSHIRE POST

"The Yorkshire Post still say before the public information both exhaustive and perfect."

FOUNDED AS THE LEEDS INTELLIGENCER, 1754

COMMENT

strapped councils at the mercy of the outdated and fatally flawed Bellwin scheme, which was created in 1983 by the former leader of Leeds City Council, to compensate local authorities in the event of an emergency.

Even though it has assisted many, Bellwin's prescriptive nature means, for example, that councils can only reclaim 85 per cent of clean-up costs incurred within the first two months of a disaster. Even this is a bureaucratic and time-consuming procedure. It does not cover the actual

cost of repairing schools, public buildings, roads, drains and sewers that have suffered so much damage.

It does not provide the mechanism to assist individuals who were uninsured; many because insurance companies refuse to provide affordable levels of cover in high-risk areas.

And it does not give local authorities the financial scope needed to build long-delayed flood prevention schemes.

Ministers, nevertheless, continue to hide behind Bellwin as if it was a fool-proof solution rather than being demonstrably part of the problem.

This complacency ignores the fact that climate change, and the absence of adequate storm drains and such like, has left virtually every community in Yorkshire at risk – even more so as weather forecasters start to gloomily predict further flooding this autumn because there will be insufficient time for flood plains and sodden fields to drain off and dry out. As such, there is little comfort to be drawn from the Government's decision

to increase flooding and coastal defence spending to £800m in three years' time. This meagre sum will barely cover Yorkshire's needs, never mind those of the entire country.

It is also perverse that Ministers are reluctant to apply for European aid when compensation has been liberally paid to countries on the Continent that have suffered far less damage than Yorkshire.

And nor should the Government be allowed to divert money away from crucial economic regeneration schemes to pay for the mop-up operation.

To do so is not only unacceptable, but would also exacerbate the difficulties of economically deprived areas – many of which have borne the brunt of recent storms and are now confronted by a growing health hazard.

Practical help and financial assistance for flooded communities must go to the top of Gordon Brown's political agenda.

If it doesn't, both the Prime Minister – and his government – will be guilty of a basic dereliction of duty.

12-PAGE SPECIAL PULL-OUT SUPPLEMENT

INSIDE: The devastation of our region P2-3 ● **How people are putting their lives back together** P4-5 ● **Stories from those caught up in the chaos** P6-9 ● **The expert opinion** P10-11 ● **Where and why the floods wreaked havoc** P12

Scene of devastation: This aerial view of the village of Catcliffe, near Sheffield, serves a stark reminder of the day the rains came to Yorkshire and the suffering the water brought with it for thousands of people.

The Great Flood The day of devastation

How rain brought death

> I do accept that the system was overwhelmed... but when you get rainfall of this character, even the best defences in the world may be overtopped and overwhelmed sometimes, and it's not the fault of the arrangements that were in place.
>
> Environment Secretary
> **Hilary Benn**

> Hull is rapidly becoming the forgotten victim of the floods that have happened across the country. The Environment Agency and Government office have told me Hull is the worst-hit place in the country.
>
> Leader of Hull City Council
> **Carl Minns**

> I've been in the fire service for 29 and a half years and I've never seen anything like it before.
>
> Firefighter, Calderdale district manager
> **David Gardiner**

> Every room is taken. It's difficult for people because they don't know whether to book for two weeks or a month.
>
> General manager at Holiday Inn, Hull Marina
> **Sarah Whitfield**

> We are looking at a bill of £10,000 to £15,000. I don't know if or when we will be going back home.
>
> Sheffield flood victim
> **Carl Harris**

Mark Branagan

AT first it seemed like just another rainy summer's day – until age-old services ground to a halt and whole populations found themselves trapped in rising water.

Soon, thousands in Yorkshire's industrial heartlands were living as people in more rural hotspots in North and East Yorkshire had lived years ago – with eyes on river levels and storm clouds, wondering if the next downpour could trigger disaster.

Sheffield found itself virtually marooned after days of chaos in which more than 100 people were airlifted to safety by search and rescue helicopters.

Offices, factories and homes were deluged, leaving workers and residents trapped or stranded.

Even the city's monument to its own Renaissance – the Meadowhall shopping centre – was swamped.

But two in Sheffield paid the ultimate price – Peter Harding, 68, was caught in floodwaters and 14-year-old Ryan Joe Parry fell into the River Sheaf at Millhouses.

A third life was lost in Hull despite a four-hour battle to rescue the victim from neck high water.

Mike Barnett, 28, later died of hypothermia after getting his foot trapped in a storm drain he was trying to mend in Hessle.

In Hull, the devastation was particularly severe and the community would later complain of inadequate Government response and that it had become the "Forgotten City" of one of Britain's worst peacetime disasters.

There was mayhem across the region as rivers burst their banks and flooded homes and businesses – or torrents of rainwater swept through communities simply because the ground was so saturated it had nowhere else to go.

It was not just big communities such as Doncaster and Rotherham which were hit. Pickering also paid a heavy price for the decision to shelve its flood defences when the beck burst its banks – pushing up the number of homes affected in North Yorkshire to 400.

The 999 services approached meltdown point, and many made homeless found there was no room at the inn as queues for rooms started building outside hotels in devastated areas.

Nearly two weeks on, the water in parts of Doncaster is still to go down before people can even return to their homes to assess the damage.

Only now as the true futures of those affected emerge – and grow bigger by the day – can the real scale of the disaster be seen.

Nearly 40,000 people in the region are feared homeless – including an estimated 20,000 in Hull, 3,000 in the East Riding, 1,000 in Rotherham, and 1,200 in Barnsley.

Some victims have lost everything having fled in the clothes they stood up in and could face being without a permanent roof over their heads until well after next Christmas.

Sinking fast: Above, a rubbish bin bobs by the tops of two cars just seen above the waters of the River Don after it flooded Meadow Hall Road, Sheffield. Below left, water on railway tracks at Mexborough, near Rotherham. Below right, drivers negotiate the flooded A63 dual carriageway near Brough, in East Yorkshire.

Three perish as the true human cost of this disaster is brought home in South Yorkshire and Hull

Mike Barnett: Died after getting trapped in a drain.

RYAN PARRY, 14, was the youngest victim of the floods.

The teenager fell into the River Sheaf in Millhouses Park, Sheffield, as he was walking home from school.

Ryan had to go home from King Egbert School in Dore on foot on Monday, June 25, as his normal bus was not running because of the conditions. He fell in and was dragged under by the swirling current.

His parents Mandy and Chris, of Gleadless, Sheffield, said he was a "kind boy who always put everyone before himself".

His funeral was held at Gleadless Methodist Church yesterday.

Peter Harding was swept away in a torrent of water beneath a railway bridge in the Lower Don Valley, Sheffield, as the area was engulfed by flood water. People were forced to grab hold of girders to save their lives, but the 68-year-old slipped down underneath the water.

A passer by tried desperately to pull Mr Harding out, but sadly he did not survive. The hero calmly took off his coat and handed it to an onlooker before diving straight in to the deep, fast-flowing water. He dragged Mr Harding out and tried to revive him. The tragedy happened on June 25.

The 45-year-old man, who only wanted to be identified as Darren, later said: "Peter didn't look his age. He looked younger than me, and I was living in hope that he'd made it through."

Mike Barnett died of hypothermia after getting his foot trapped in a storm drain he was trying to mend in Hessle, near Hull.

The 28-year-old was stuck in neck-high water for almost four hours as emergency services workers battled to save him. Eventually, he was freed but he lost consciousness and died shortly afterwards on Monday, June 25. At the beginning of the crisis one neighbour dived down several times to try to free Mr Barnett but without success. Firefighters then attempted to cut the grate, which was actually a piece of fencing material put in place after the original grille was damaged in previous flooding. It is thought Mr Barnett got his foot trapped in the makeshift metal grille as he tried to clear some debris.

Mr Barnett's family have also complained not enough was done to save him.

Humberside's chief fire officer Frank Duffield said the crews acted in a "dedicated and professional manner"

Ryan Parry: Was the youngest victim of the floods.

| The levels on the Rivers Don and Dearne in South Yorkshire are the highest ever recorded. | At its peak, the Environment Agency had 14 severe flood warnings across Yorkshire region. | More than 8,000 insurance claims were received in the first 24 hours after the floods hit the county. | Almost 40,000 people from across the Yorkshire region are now homeless. | 400 million tonnes of water fell in the Humber, South Yorkshire and West Yorkshire regions in just 12 hours. | This is the equivalent of 18 Olympic swimming pools of water falling every second. | Hull suffered a sixth of its expected annual rainfall, 100mm, in the space of just 12 hours. |

"I've been in the fire service for 29 and a half years and I've never seen anything like it."

Sinking fast: A rubbish bin bobs by the tops of two cars just seen above the waters of the River Don after it flooded Meadow Hall Road, Sheffield.

(below left) Water on railway tracks at Mexborough, near Rotherham.

(below right) Drivers negotiated the flooded A63 dual carriageway near Brough, in East Yorkshire.

www.yorkshirepost.co.uk · SPECIAL PUBLICATION SATURDAY JULY 7 2007 · **3**

The Great Flood The day of devastation

and misery to our region

What a day: Fire crews, above, rescue motorists from their vehicles on the main A62 trunk road in Leeds while there were even more dramatic scenes in South Yorkshire where an RAF helicopter, left, was scrambled to winch stranded people to safety. However, it was not only the human lives which were in danger as people in New Farnley, right, proved when they rescued their chickens from the rising flood waters.

> If plans were already in place to conduct an appraisal for Sheffield's flood defences, then this flooding should give an overwhelming reason to bring that study forward.
>
> Liberal Democrat MP for Sheffield Hallam
> **Nick Clegg**

> We have had another wake-up call that we have got to do more to adapt to the changing climate and that includes adapting more through the planning system as well as providing investment in flood defences.
>
> Chairman of the Yorkshire Flood Defence Committee
> **Jeremy Walker**

> People no longer see natural disasters as acts of Gods. However, we are now reaping what we have sown.
>
> Bishop of Liverpool and former Bishop of Hull
> **Rt Rev James Jones**

> Retaining walls are collapsing, several have come down and some of these walls are 100 years old. There's no way of getting out.
>
> Trapped in Brightside Lane, Sheffield
> **Phil Davies**

> I will do everything possible to secure additional assistance as it is required.
>
> Sheffield Brightside MP
> **David Blunkett**

JOIN OUR FIGHT FOR FUNDS

WE need your help to make the Government give a firm pledge of money to help Yorkshire's flood-hit communities.

On our website you'll find an online petition calling for direct, urgent action to bring relief where it's needed, right now. The more people who sign it, the more weight it will carry.

It will take just a few seconds but could make a big difference. Please log on to www.yorkshirepost.co.uk /flooding and sign it today.

We also want to know what has happened to you and your family.

Are you struggling to rebuild your life or business, find a new home or do you want to highlight how friends and neighbours have rallied round?

Let us know by clicking on the same address.

You will also find a complete archive of our floods coverage, including picture galleries and reports on video.

You can also send us your pictures, videos, stories and texts – you'll find all the details online.

yorkshirepost.co.uk
Get involved now by logging on to our website and you could help make a difference.

Threat of further problems as country is left saturated

FEARS that Yorkshire could see more devastating flooding this autumn are growing with forecasters now predicting that last month's floods could lead to worse problems.

In June 2000 flash flooding hit parts of Yorkshire such as Todmorden, leaving the ground saturated.

When far greater rain fell in the autumn that year the soaked ground could not take in any more water, flooding swathes of Yorkshire, including York which was left under water for days.

Now weather experts are worried the same fate may fall again this year – on an even greater scale.

Forecasters say if we don't get a dry spell over the summer months and there is a wet autumn, more communities face a repeat of the past two weeks.

With the relentless rain continuing there appears little chance of a quick solution.

The possibility of more flooding piles on the pressure for action to be taken now to improve defences across Yorkshire.

A spokesman for the Environment Agency said that it would study long-term forecasts from the Met Office but that it would not comment on a "how long is a piece of string" scenario.

The Met Office said that June had been the wettest on record with 140.2mm falling on average throughout England, smashing the previous 1997 high by almost 20mm.

Those figures were far higher in Yorkshire, which saw 103.1mm falling on June 15 at Fylingdales, North Yorkshire, alone.

"At this stage, it is not possible to say whether intense rainfall events are caused by climate change. However, there is an expectation of heavier extreme rainfall events in most places as climate warms and the atmosphere becomes more moist," a spokesman said.

Firefighters across Yorkshire received more than 4,000 emergency calls in less than a week.	Last week Humberside Fire and Rescue had 3,227 calls. It had 376 this period last year.	Seventeen fire crews pumped a total of 8.5m litres of water an hour from the Ulley Dam.	Some of the biggest pumps in Europe removed water from the worst-hit areas of South Yorkshire.	At Toll Bar, 24 high-volume pumps continue to pump away 14m litres of water an hour.	A total of three hundred people were eventually airlifted to safety across the South Yorkshire region.	Four RAF helicopters from Leconfield, Bulmer and Wattisham carried out rescues.	

"People no longer see natural disasters as acts of Gods ... We are reaping what we have sown."

What a day: Fire crews rescued motorists from their vehicles on the main A62 trunk road in Leeds.

(lower left) Dramatic scenes in South Yorkshire where an RAF helicopter was scrambled to winch stranded people to safety.

(right) Chickens rescued from the rising flood in New Farnley.

The Great Flood The cost of rebuilding

Defence is best form of attack in future

New ways must be found to stop water

Tom Smithard

WHOLE swathes of Yorkshire need new flood defences installed to prevent torrential downpours causing the same havoc each year.

Previous schemes built in the region have protected against the threat of flooding from the sea and rivers – but nothing was in place to cope with the sheer scale of water that descended over Yorkshire on June 25.

Areas such as Sheffield, built on hills and with no need for flood defence works in the past, were swamped with rain which overwhelmed Victorian drainage systems, culminating in the chaos that cost three lives.

It was the same type of flash flooding 10 days earlier which saw much of North and West Yorkshire under water and cost the life of a soldier stationed at Catterick garrison.

Now attention is turning towards the flood defences and sewerage work the region will need to help prevent further loss of life and damage stretching into billions of pounds.

John Mothersole, Sheffield Council deputy chief executive, said the city had entered new territory with the flooding, which had exposed all its weak points.

He said: "Even if what happened last Monday was a freak event, that's not to say rain in future won't be nearly as bad and we need a system capable of dealing with surface drainage.

"We have never had investment in flood defences,

"We have never had investment in flood defences, we've not needed them. But this is new territory."

we've not needed them, but this is new territory.

"We need to look at the height and nature of all our bridges – our flat bridges are not high enough to cope with swollen rivers and act as dams, worsening an already bad situation. Raising bridges will cost a vast sum of money, but everything's changed now and we need to react to that."

In Rotherham, council leaders said there was ongoing investment in flood defence work, but that there was a lot more still to be done to protect the district.

Bag men: Council workers put sandbags on the roads in Bentley, near Doncaster, as flood waters continue to rise. Now there are calls for more permanent measures to be introduced so that flooding can be avoided in future years.

Chief executive Mike Cuff said that he would be pushing the Government to fund more work to strengthen defences in the town centre and build them in places elsewhere in the borough that were flooded last week.

In Hull, a city 95 per cent under the coast line, all flood defences have been geared up to dealing with rising levels in the Humber Estuary.

But Hull Council chief executive Kym Ryley said that the city now also faced a very different threat.

"We have flood defences based on tidal surge as that's what people have been worried about in the past. What we had was something very different, where the normal drainage systems were overwhelmed by the scale and speed of rainfall. We now need different infrastructure to be able to cope."

Leeds City Council will be lobbying the Government to invest £100m in a scheme to build flood defences along the River Aire, protecting the city centre from a repeat of last Monday's floods.

The scheme has been under development by the Environment Agency for a number of years but was recently shelved as a result of financial constraints. Councillors are also calling for the Agency to build a flood defence scheme for Wyke Beck, where 30 households had to be evacuated for the third time in three years.

Leader Mark Harris said: "We can't turn a blind eye to changing weather patterns. We have had significant floods in parts of the city for four years now and our drainage system wasn't built to deal with the levels of rainfall we are now experiencing.

"We understand that the Agency has enormous pressures from around the country for flood defences but we honestly believe the situation in Leeds is very serious and needs immediate attention.

"Over the next few weeks we will be making this absolutely clear to the Government to ensure that action is taken to tackle the issue as a matter of urgency."

It is a similar story in North Yorkshire, where an £11 7m scheme for Ripon was shelved in March 2006, three months after being given initial approval.

It was intended to protect 600 homes and businesses and was expected to have been built by now.

In 2004, a £6.7m scheme to protect homes in Pickering was postponed and has yet to be built. Pickering and Ripon were two of the towns in North Yorkshire that suffered in last week's flooding.

Robin Myshrall, head of emergency planning at North Yorkshire Council, said: "Previously our flood season lasted November to March but this is something very different. In places such as Selby 150 properties were flooded by surface water, nothing to do with rivers at all. We know what parts of rivers will flood and can plan against that when levels are high but with flash flooding the water cannot be drained away and that can happen anywhere.

"With 3,100 square miles in our county that can be somewhat of a problem.

"Areas are being flooded before we're even hearing about it, making it impossible to get sandbags out in time.

"We're playing catch up. The amount of resources we'd have to have on standby to deal with this is somewhat of an issue."

Farmers' fears as valuable crops lie ruined

Robert Benson
Agricultural Correspondent

FARMERS across Yorkshire are facing a new crisis as thousands of acres still lie under water.

A nightmare scenario is facing pea growers. Britain's harvest of peas – the biggest in Europe – has been devastated by the weather, with as much as 50,000 tonnes of the annual crop of 150,000 tonnes expected to be lost.

It is estimated that 25 per cent of the crop in Yorkshire has been ruined and some growers in East Yorkshire are looking at 60 per cent of their crops being completely written off.

In a good year the pea crop, in Yorkshire is estimated at £15m.

The National Farmers' Union is calling on the Government to look at how similar scenes of devastation can be prevented. The organisation is already in serious talks with the Environment Agency on the way that rivers and drainage dykes are being managed.

The unprecedented deluge will come under the spotlight on Tuesday when the Great Yorkshire Show opens for a three-day run at Harrogate.

With the cereals harvest just around the corner the severe wet weather could not have come at a worse time.

Hay and silage making in some areas has also been affected, not just in terms of timing, but in quality and quantity.

This will lead to a shortage of winter livestock feed.

Pick-your-own farms have also been badly affected with a loss of trade, while vegetable growers in Lincolnshire and South Yorkshire, two of the major growing areas are facing diabolical conditions.

And the rain has badly hit the planting of cabbage and sprouts for harvest in the autumn.

Weather-damaged fruit and arable crops are standing in water, leading to fears of reduced quality once the cereal harvest gets under way.

National Farmers' Union (NFU) president, Peter Kendal, who visited a number of farms around Doncaster, said he had never seen a situation where cereal crops were totally submerged.

NFU vice-president, Paul Temple, who grows peas on his farm near Driffield, said: "We had two months of rainfall here in 13 hours and peas are particularly sensitive to waterlogged soils. Any longer than 24 hours and it effectively kills the crop."

Farmers are also suffering particular problems with flooded fields of potatoes and there are serious concerns especially where crops are completely submerged.

"The main problems now facing the industry is potato blight and other fungal diseases which are brought on by warm, wet weather."

Farm fears: This aerial view of the M1 near Rotherham, pictured while it was closed after two days of heavy rain, shows how the floods badly affected the countryside. Some farmland remains under water and many crops have already been ruined.

yorkshirepost.co.uk
Please sign our petition and help us to force the Government to help the flood-hit communities across Yorkshire. You can send us your comments and view a complete archive of our floods coverage, including reports on video, at: www.yorkshirepost.co.uk/flooding

Businesses warned they face a long, hard road back

SEVERAL thousand businesses are likely to have been affected by the flooding – with agencies now engaged in a long-term battle to keep as many solvent as possible.

It is not just those who suffer water damage which close, but also those further up or down the supply chain which rely on businesses directly hit.

Directors of regional development agency Yorkshire Forward said they were working closely with larger businesses affected, liaising with chambers of commerce, and had set up a help line to advise smaller businesses caught up in the flooding.

A £1m fund put in place last week, which provides grants of up to £2,500 to help businesses with short-term costs, has already received more than 1,000 hits on its website and 500 calls to a dedicated line.

Don Stewart, director of strategy and tasked with taking charge of the response to the flooding, said: "It's difficult to get a hand on the exact numbers of businesses affected but there are indications there will be several thousand affected.

"Some will be directly affected and others will be further along the supply chain. Research shows that many businesses shut down, either because they weren't insured or because they just didn't think it was worthwhile starting up again."

Mr Stewart said Yorkshire Forward were doing everything they could to keep the region's bigger companies in business, such as helping one South Yorkshire firm offload staff to another business on a short-term loan until it was able to get off the ground again.

He said that the agency was not just hoping businesses would ask for help, but was working with the Post Office to identify and then target those that appeared to be out of action.

"Typically, it can take a year to find out exactly what the cost to business is.

"We'll have a clearer picture in terms of numbers in about three months but it's far too early to estimate what the damage to Yorkshire's economy will be."

"There are a lot of businesses which have already got themselves back up and running again.

"Especially in South Yorkshire there's been a lot of resilience, businesses are showing some real Yorkshire grit."

FLOOD FACTS

- Damage to roads in Hull will cost £50-60m to put right, with another £50-60m for schools.
- Damage in Sheffield will cost "millions and millions" to repair.
- About £7m of damage done to homes in Leeds.
- Floods will have cost Network Rail about £10m.
- Damage to Yorkshire Water equipment will cost "millions" to put right.
- 52 schools affected in Doncaster.
- Defence schemes for Pickering and Ripon costing £18.4m were shelved – both places flooded last week.
- Only 46 per cent of flood defence schemes nationally were judged up-to-standard early last month.
- Research shows it can cost up to £40,000 per household to repair damage.
- 40 per cent of small businesses closed by flooding do not start up again.

"We can't turn a blind eye to changing weather patterns... Action must be taken."

Bag men: Council workers put sandbags on the roads in Bentley, near Doncaster, as flood waters continued to rise.

(bottom) This aerial view of the M1 near Rotherham, pictured while it was closed after two days of heavy rain, shows how the floods badly affected the countryside. Many crops were ruined.

www.yorkshirepost.co.uk — SPECIAL PUBLICATION SATURDAY JULY 7 2007 — 5

The Great Flood The cost of rebuilding

The waters may at last be receding across the county but only now is the true cost of the floods coming to light

Before: The picture tells the tale as flood waters engulfed the centre of Catcliffe in Rotherham, causing damage estimated at millions of pounds to the area and bringing chaos to the submerged streets.

Search is on to find missing millions

Tom Smithard

REBUILDING swathes of Yorkshire damaged by the floods will cost hundreds of millions of pounds - and with no Government funding in sight, could knock the region's regeneration plans back by a generation.

Huge parts of Hull, Sheffield, Rotherham and Doncaster need rebuilding, along with many other towns and villages throughout North, South, East and West Yorkshire.

In Hull, about 15,000 homes were flooded and, with the majority of the city under the water line, it is likely many more will have been damaged by water flowing under the houses and into the foundations.

With an average wage of about £15,000, many in the city do not have insurance and will not be able to afford repairs.

Almost all of the city's schools were flooded and most have their boiler systems in their basement - which will need costly repairs before autumn.

Council chief executive Kym Ryley said it was too early to give definitive costs for the repair work but that it could cost about £68m to get schools and leisure centres operable again.

He said: "We're worried we're being overlooked. I'm not convinced there's still a clear understanding from London of the scale of problems in Yorkshire, they're all underplaying it.

"Our need is pretty urgent. It will take at least £50 – £60m to repair our schools and the same amount again to rebuild our roads.

"If we start appropriating capital we've committed to regeneration projects then the city will go backwards, and that will not be helpful."

The council has not yet received any guarantees from Government about long-term funding.

They have already had to divert £50m away from a £35m package of spending improvements on council homes into repairing short-term damage such as preventing mould that would in time cause houses to rot.

"It can't be sensible to force any northern city that's trying to regenerate itself to pay for the damage sustained. We need a clear commitment of financial support," he said.

In Sheffield, the most pressing problem is repairing the roads - many of which, like the A6102 Millwood Road, have collapsed. A further 300 houses were flooded.

John Mothersole, deputy chief executive, said: "The damage done to Sheffield runs into millions and millions of pounds. The main cost will be repairing our road network, stopping bridges from collapsing and roads from deteriorating further.

"So far there have been no signs from the Government that funding will be forthcoming. But this is not a time for knee-jerk reactions

to calls for long-term investment."

Doncaster Mayor Martin Winter said that the infrastructure damage seen elsewhere in South Yorkshire has not been so great in his town, where flooding was caused by rivers breaking their banks rather than a torrential downpour.

He said the true cost would be seen in hidden damage – and with most of the district built on flood plains it could force the relocation of communities on a massive scale. We're going to have to look at really radical solutions.

"With 75 per cent of Toll Bar damaged we might have to move the whole community to higher ground and we'll have to consider ceasing building on flood plains completely.

"Just as important are the hidden costs. We have 24,000 pupils in 52 schools affected by this and we are very worried that their educational attainment will slip.

"We're also going to have to landfill thousands of tonnes of waste and we are very concerned we will be penalised for that.

"It's important the Government understand that the impact on the communities of South Yorkshire is as much more than the costs that the Bellwin funding offered will cover."

After: The clean-up continues in the centre of Catcliffe days after the roads were completely under water. The floods may have gone in some areas, but the hard work is just beginning for many people.

Mike Cuff, chief executive of Rotherham Council, said it was still trying to get a full assessment of the full scale of the damage but that it would certainly be "in the millions"

He said: "The bill will be significant. There are issues about the Bellwin money being promised to councils not including money needed for capital investment, and we need to get into urgent discussions with the Government around that.

"We will need some help for repairing the infrastructure, which has seen significant damage to schools, roads and several hundred properties.

ments to calculate the true cost of the floods. In terms of cost to the council, such as staffing, equipment, sandbags, damage to roads, we're talking about hundreds of thousands of pounds.

"With the average cost of repairing flooded properties being £26,000, the 250 proper ties flooded in Leeds will cost £7m.

"And the economic impact to the city will also be significant, with people leaving early, not coming in the next day, and damage to businesses - including the train station - likely to run into several millions of pounds."

But it is not just home-owners and councils out of pocket because of the floods – most companies responsible for the region's infrastructure have been hit hard as well.

Rachel Lowe, spokeswoman for Network Rail, said: "We are still trying to calculate the exact costs but they will be about £10m.

"Most of that will go as compensation to train operating companies unable to run services, though a significant proportion will be spent on repairing infrastructure, including in excess of £1m at Kiverton, near Sheffield, where track was left hanging in mid-air in places."

A spokeswoman for the Environment Agency's North-East team, based in Leeds, said work would begin in the near future to repair damaged river banks.

some privately owned, some publicly. There are also issues around business recovery, it is important businesses are not forgotten."

Elsewhere in the region, road rebuilding was also high on this list of priorities, with North Yorkshire Council having patched up many routes – including parts of the A59 – but which will soon need expensive long-term repair work.

Ministers struggle to come up with answers

Tom Smithard

IN Parliamentary statements, media interviews and visits to people and councils affected by the flooding, Ministers have promised two sources of money: Bellwin and the social fund.

Both have been criticised by opposition MPs and backbenchers in flooded constituencies, the latter as inappropriate and the former as not going far enough. Instead, they say the Government should take the extraordinary step of applying for a grant from the Regional Solidarity Fund – something Britain has never successfully managed to do before.

In a Statement to Parliament this week, Environment Secretary and Leeds Central MP Hilary Benn said that insurance costs would run to £1bn but the cost to councils would be covered by Bellwin funding, available after major emergencies.

He said: "The costs to local authorities of responding to the flooding will be covered by the long-established Bellwin arrangements. The money that will go to local authorities through the Bellwin scheme will depend on the costs that they incur, so I cannot give an estimate at this point."

But Bellwin only covers 85 per cent of costs and can

only be used for immediate, short-term repairs to infrastructure to restore stability - not the far more important and costly long-term repairs to damaged flood defence schemes and roads.

Damage sustained during flooding in Carlisle in January 2005 cost £7.9m to repair – yet the funding made available via Bellwin

"We may need to look at the issue of creating a hardship fund."

amounted to a mere £400,000. On a visit to stricken communities in Toll Bar, near Doncaster, Mr Benn told the Yorkshire Post that he would be talking to Work and Pensions Secretary Peter Hain about releasing money from the Government's social fund to help those who have lost everything. In Parliament he announced that £170m would be made available through crisis loans, having been shocked to find that half the people he met in Toll Bar did not have insurance.

But on a visit to Leeds, Tory leader David Cameron said the social fund, which helps people on a low income to pay for one-off

expenses such as winter fuel bills or maternity cover, was not the appropriate source.

He said: "Of course, people should have insurance, but we may need to look at the issue of creating a special hardship fund."

Mr Benn has also announced that the Environment Agency would be given an extra £200m of funding a year from 2010/11 to pay for flood defences, its budget rising from £600m to £800m.

But under questioning from Liberal Democrat environment spokesman Chris Hulme, Mr Benn refused to say whether there would be any increase in funding.

Familiar tale: The people of Carlisle received only a fraction of the true cost of rebuilding their lives.

"We are going to have to look at radical solutions ... The community may move."

The picture tells the tale as flood waters engulfed the centre of Catcliffe in Rotherham, causing damage estimated at millions of pounds to the area and bringing chaos to the submerged streets.

The Great Flood The people's stories – Sheffield

A Royal mess: Prince Charles, with Forgemasters chief executive Dr Graham Honeyman, sees first hand the devastation caused in the south machine shop at Sheffield Forgemasters.

Rented housing is only solution

Rob Preece

FLOOD water swept across Sheffield within hours, but residents will have to wait months before their lives are back to normal.

Areas worst affected by the deluge include Meadowhall, the Wicker, Hillsborough and Middlewood, where residents on the Winn Garden estate had to be evacuated.

Many householders now face an anxious wait for insurance payments. Others have no insurance at all. Betty L'Amey, whose home in Penistone Road, Hillsborough, was flooded, doubts she will receive any help from the Government.

She said: "It's something I don't want anyone else to go through. It's a nightmare. Everything's gone. What do the Government do? What do they ever do? Look after the rich."

Ms L'Amey's home now houses two dehumidifiers, but the stench caused by the flood water is almost unbearable.

She said: "The whole place is stinking. All the furniture is damaged and the fireplace is coming away from the wall.

"We've both had operations recently, my husband and I, and now everything's gone. I'm in a lot of pain.

"We've tried to clean up, but it's been impossible to get contractors. So much needs doing."

Forgemasters facing huge bill for repairs

Rob Preece

SHEFFIELD Forgemasters like many businesses is now facing a huge repair bill – and staff are counting the personal cost of the disaster.

Conservative estimates put the firm's repair bill at £10m and the major employers is in crisis again, less than three years after it was on the brink of closure.

Thirty staff are unlikely to forget the night they spent in a powerless factory, unable to get out because of the floods. Another 20 employees were airlifted to safety by an RAF helicopter as flood water gushed relentlessly below.

Dozens more staff lost their cars, some of which were discovered a mile away from the factory when the clean-up operation began.

One employee saw his new £30,000 Jaguar saloon car destroyed. He had bought the car using money left by his late mother, who had died just two weeks before the flooding came.

Director Peter Birtles said: "It was a very high-pressure situation and a time of desperation for some people.

"Everybody's insured, but those who've got third party insurance have taken a loss and those who are fully comp have lost their excess and their no claims bonus."

The flooding has interrupted a period of recovery for the company, which has 700 staff and was threatened with closure before a management buyout was agreed.

Mr Birtles said: "Up to about three years ago, it was on the brink of closure. It was a depressing time for everybody.

"A new management buyout went through in September 2005 and, during the two-year period since, people have seen a massive recovery, with a big increase in the order book and a big recruitment campaign.

"Suddenly, this deluge happened. There was a real sense of having coming back from the brink to a couple of years ago, getting to a place where we had a real future, and then that optimism being dashed in this flood."

The flooding also had disastrous consequences for national charity Support Dogs, which trains dogs for disabled people at its Brightside Lane headquarters.

A wall on the Forgemasters site came crashing down on the building, causing structural damage which will take months to repair. The £300,000 centre opened two years ago, following a 13-year fundraising drive, and it could be six months before staff return.

Manager Amanda Hutt, of Chapeltown, Sheffield, said: "We help people who are completely dependent on other people, don't have any time on their own, and can't get out of their home. It gives them their life back.

"All of us at Support Dogs are not there because its our job; it's more than that. It's our blood, sweat and tears that we've put in during weekends and evenings, and the fundraising that's gone in in our own time.

"We left work on the Monday and, when we returned on the Tuesday, we had nothing left."

Listening in: Prince Charles talks to workers at Sheffield Forgemasters, one of the businesses worst hit by the floods.

Tide trouble: Cars float alongside the Sheffield Forgemasters factory after the downpour.

Shopping mall still affected

MORE than 100 shops at the region's biggest shopping mall remain closed.

Bosses at Meadowhall shopping centre, in Sheffield, are still totting up the cost of the deluge, but the sum is expected to run into "seven figures".

The entire mall was closed for six days after the flood, and it could be two months before some stores re-open.

About 150 of the centre's 270 shops have reopened, but the lower level of the Oasis food court and the Vue cinema will not re-open for another two to four weeks.

A Meadowhall spokesman said: "Up to 140 or 150 shops are open in total, and that is improving on a daily basis.

"All the upper level is fine with shops trading as usual, and on the lower level we have about 40 or 50 trading as normal. The rest are boarded up, and the timescale for them re-opening ranges between a week and eight weeks. Some stores are doing complete refits, while others are just doing some interior decorating."

Major retailers Debenhams, Next, House of Fraser and Marks and Spencer have resumed trading, but other big names such as BHS and H&M remain closed.

After the downpour...

Under water: Neither Hillsborough, above left, or the Meadowhall Shopping Centre, above right, could escape the torrent of water. Centre, an evacuee takes shelter at Dinnington Comprehensive School.

"It was a high-pressure situation and a time of desperation for some people."

The Great Flood The people's stories – South Yorkshire

Refuges do their best to offer support but the reality of life after the floods is just beginning to dawn

Families forced to start all over again

Martin Slack

JOHN EMMERSON spent £10,000 improving his house - a new conservatory, new windows and a new kitchen all helped make it a real home from home.

Now he has no choice but to start from scratch – when he returned to Toll Bar this week his brand new floor was floating around the kitchen.

Mr Emmerson and his daughter Gemma, 24, whose baby is one today, have no insurance after being refused following several burglaries. They are staying in council refuges and do not know where they will live in future or have any clue where they will go.

As Sheffield flooded, people in Doncaster know what came next.

They knew that the water was rushing somewhere, and they saw that millions of gallons were being pumped out of a reservoir at Ulley, near Rotherham. They saw that the water would end up in the River Don.

They knew there was going to be a flood, but could never have foreseen just how bad that flood was going to be.

By the early hours of Wednesday morning, hundreds of people were wondering what to do as the water got higher and higher, but no word came from the police, council or other authorities.

Railway worker Mr Emmerson, 58, said: "When the flood got really bad we were just sitting here, wondering what was happening. I didn't want to leave in case of looters. The police have said it isn't happening but a lot of people around have would disagree.

"It was horrible when I came back – it is going to be no place for a baby. Nobody gave us any warning of what was going to happen - it was all word of mouth. My daughter rang the police and they said it might be an idea to evacuate. Look at it now."

> **"It was horrible when I came back – it is going to be no place for a baby... Nobody warned us."**

A few doors up the road, Claire Didcott, 34, and her family decided to stay in their home and live upstairs with knee-deep water in the lounge and kitchen.

Mrs Didcott, who lives with her groundworker husband Stephen, 37, and their two sons Nathan, 11, and Matthew, eight, is on immuno-suppressant drugs following a kidney transplant.

"The drugs are supposed to stop me rejecting the kidney but I am much more susceptible to infections because of them," said the teaching assistant, who was at Toll Bar Primary School when a call came through from the council to send the children home.

"It was very worrying to have contaminated water flowing through my house. We decided to stay, but it has been like camping in your own house. We have been able to use the gas hob and my husband bought a generator from a DIY shop so its been OK, but we don't know who is going to help with the clean up."

Next door, devastated single mum Dawn Haslam has been examining the damage the water had done to her home, which she had single-handedly renovated, laying new floors and redecorating throughout.

Miss Haslam, who lives in the house with her three children Jade, 14, Carly, 13, and Joshua, eight, added

"The water has been about four feet deep in my house. It has wrecked the entire ground floor.

"I thought I was insured, but when I phoned the insurance company they told me I had no cover for this kind of thing. I am living with my sister now and her children. We had booked a holiday and were due to go in two weeks.

"I think that will have to be cancelled while I try and get this mess sorted out."

Temporary home: Neil Copeland, Gemma Emmerson and one year-old Ruby have been forced to stay at the Adwick sports centre after the flood while Gemma's dad John continues to clean up the mess, right.

Cheers: Rosato Ferdinando with the glass of wine which survived two days floating in flood water.

Residents face the grim task of rebuilding their lives once more

ROSATO Ferdinando faces the grim task of rebuilding his life for a second time.

In 2000, the 48-year-old was forced out of his home in Orgreave Road, Catcliffe, after the River Don, which runs on the other side of the road, burst its banks.

Now his home has again been ruined and he is living in the Holiday Inn at Canklow, Rotherham, until his insurance company can decide what to do with the house.

Looking around his lounge, the 48-year-old said that all his furniture had floated around the room, with the three-piece suite lying on its back and kitchen appliances which were under worktops standing in the middle of the kitchen.

Before he left, he had been drinking a bottle of wine, and had left a full glass on the coffee table. It was the only thing intact, having survived by floating around the room on the coffee table where he left it.

Mr Ferdinando, who runs the La Taverna restaurant in Sheffield's Meadowhead, said: "I moved into this house in May 1999, the year after that I was flooded. It was horrendous. Everything was ruined. So when the water started creeping up again we were praying for it to stay out.

"The previous Friday there was heavy rain and the water had come up to the front garden but it went away so we were relieved. But after the next rains it was worse.

"We were standing out at the front at 3am watching the water get closer and closer. Then the police came round and told us to leave because there was a danger that the dam at Ulley was going to burst."

He added: "When the flood came in 2000 the water was about four feet high, and I was hoping that it wouldn't be that bad this time around. But it has been worse. I think more than five feet of water this time. The first time around it felt really bad, I can't really describe the empty feeling. We were out for about eight months. The insurance company think it may be even longer now, and I have no idea how much it will cost."

The floods will also disrupt wedding plans for one young couple.

Mike Torr, 23, who lives with his fiancee Nadine Russell, 25, said: "We are getting married in October, but we won't be moving back in here before then. It has ruined our life for now and had a worse effect on those people who have suffered before. I hope something will be done to help us all."

After the downpour...

Boat ride: Residents use a boat to check on their house in Toll Bar, near Doncaster, above left, while Amy Meran, 18, centre left, and Jody Granger, 18, wade through waters in Bentley and a firefighter saves a dog in Toll Bar, above.

> **"We were standing at the front at 3am watching the water get closer and closer."**

(bottom left) Boat ride: Residents used a boat to check on their house in Toll Bar, near Doncaster.

(bottom centre) Amy Meran, 18, left, and Jody Granger, 18, waded through waters in Bentley.

(bottom right) A firefighter saved a dog in Toll Bar.

The Great Flood The people's stories – West/North Yorkshire

Panic stations as beck bursts banks

Residents call for help as estate suffers again

Joanne Ginley

EVERY time it rains on one Leeds estate residents begin to panic.

These floods were the third time in three years that homes on the Dunhill estate, Halton, had become submerged in the area after Wyke Beck, which runs through the estate, burst its banks.

David Davenport's home flooded for the first time in August 2004 – the force of the waters were so strong that it swept his 2tft garage off its foundations. He lost all his possessions including car pets, furniture and even knives and forks and had to move out while repairs were carried out.

Less than a year later his house was under water again and his possessions and way of life again ruined. Last week, the waters were up to chest height in his garden in Verity View but this time he was more prepared and managed to keep damage to a minimum by using sandbags and blocking up air vents into his property.

Mr Davenport said: "We cannot continue to live like this. Every time it rains we panic. What we really want is something doing with this beck to stop it flooding."

Last Monday about 70 properties were affected – many deluged for the third time – leaving residents worried about house prices and faced with high insurance premiums. Some residents can only get insurance if they agree to pay excess of between £2,000 and £6,000.

Coun Mick Lyons, who used to live on the estate, said he believes development in the area has put too much pressure on the beck. Investigations to find a solution have been ongoing for some time but Coun Lyons said urgent action must now be taken, problems cannot simply be blamed on unseasonal flash floods.

The floods hit many areas in West Yorkshire, including Mirfield, Liversedge, Wakefield, South Elmsall, Cleckheaton, Brighouse, Pontefract, Collingham, near Wetherby, parts of Leeds and Castleford. This week, Skipton and surrounding villages were also hit by flooding after torrential showers.

One of the worst hit areas was Agbrigg, near Wakefield, where residents were forced from their homes when floodwater reached four feet in places. Many roads had to be closed, schools were shut and people were without power.

Here, as in other parts of the region, people are having to come to terms with the fact that there are criminals waiting to take advantage of their misfortune.

Barbara Jewitt was forced to sleep rough in her car after her flooded home became a target for looters.

The 65-year-old, below, said: "I've been sleeping in the car. I left for five minutes the other day and as soon as I left a van came down to loot my stuff. When I came home, two policewomen were here and they told me people had been seen coming to loot. I daren't leave my house now."

Ms Jewitt, a retired council worker, struggled to find temporary accommodation as the owners of the dogs, who are being looked after by friends. All of her chickens drowned.

She has lived in her Agbrigg home for 15 years – and has suffered flooding before but says the latest deluge is the worst yet and says she has just "absolutely everything". All her belongings are now scattered outside the house, making Ms Jewitt a prime target for thieves.

But she says she won't move away, and added: "I have always lived here. When you don't get the floods, it's a lovely place."

Counting the cost: Victor Buchanan, of The Ginger Pig delicatessen, clears flood-damaged goods from the shop in Market Place, Pickering.

Shop owners promise to bounce back smiling

Mark Branagan

VICTOR Buchanan had no choice but to shut up one of the newest shops in Pickering – the Ginger Pig – as the floods took their toll.

The White Swan Hotel owner took over the former Seasons deli only a few months ago with farmer Tim Wilson to bring a traditional grocers back to the market town High Street.

But The Ginger Pig was this week just another business with a closed sign in the window above the lines of sodden and misshapen sand bags which had been used in a vain attempt to defend Pickering's commercial heart when the beck broke its banks.

Mopping up his own flooded offices, Philip Benham, general manager of the North Yorkshire Moors Railway, said the hope now was to salvage something of the holiday season.

He said: "The main message is that we are back in business because people are thinking they should stay away."

Les Ward, owner of Yorkshire of Quality Paperbacks further along the floodhit Ropery was also keen to underline the message that it was business as usual – even if he is being forced to live in the upstairs of his flood-damaged home further along the street.

After escaping the floods through his backyard he initially returned to find devastation in the business he has run for 16 years. He said: "Books were floating about. I have probably lost about £4,000 to £5,000 worth of books. It was probably the first time I have ever been closed."

He got to work drying out his premises with electric and gas fires, ripping off the wallpaper to help get rid of the damp faster.

"My house was very badly affected. I lost a personal book collection and the electricity and gas does not work. Local people are horrified at what has happened," he added.

"They did not think the water could go this high and one of the frightening things is it came up so fast.

"At its worst there was about four foot of water outside – enough to wash anyone away. It came and went very fast but caused a lot of damage in those few hours."

Now his only problem is customers complaining about the heat.

Paddles away: Kenny Inman, whose school was closed, makes the most of conditions in Pickering.

Businesses shut have included the HSBC Bank, which aims to reopen on Monday, The Fortune Inn Chinese restaurant, The Station Pub, The Green Man Gallery, Mrs Rummage's Tea Shop, and Ryedale Travel.

But a notice in Ryedale Travel's window sums up the spirit of the traders: "We are sorry for the inconvenience. But we will reopen, better, brighter and smiling – honest."

It would also take more than a spot of rain to stop Andrea and David Murphy, from South Cave, near Hull, enjoying their annual holiday in the area. Mrs Murphy said: "We always come every year – and anyway, we know the flood damage will be no worse than in Hull."

"We are sorry for the inconvenience. But we will reopen, better, brighter and smiling – honest."

After the downpour...

Rising waters: A horse is rescued in New Farnley, Leeds, as flood waters rise, above left. A man carries a woman through the Leeds streets, above centre, while Christine Slowther, of Bridge Cottage, Sinnington, surveys the damage.

"I've been sleeping in the car ... I daren't leave my house because of the looters."

(middle)
Paddles away: Kenny Inman, whose school was closed, made the most of conditions in Pickering.

(bottom left) A horse was rescued in New Farnley, Leeds, as flood waters rose.

(bottom centre) A piggy-backride through the streets of Leeds keeps this young woman dry.

(bottom right) Christine Slowther, of Bridge Cottage, Sinnington, surveyed the damage.

www.yorkshirepost.co.uk   SPECIAL PUBLICATION SATURDAY JULY 7 2007   9

The Great Flood The people's stories – East Yorkshire

Local offers solace in torrid times

Simon Bristow

Flood-hit residents take time out for a morale-boosting drink

IT was raining at 6am on Monday, June 25, when Kevin Orton pulled out of his drive in Knightley Way, Kingswood, and left for work.

He had not travelled far before he was fielding a call from concerned wife Tracey, to say the water was coming up the house was flooding.

At 8am she rang again to say the water was coming up the drive.

"I said 'Don't worry, the drains are there, they'll cope with it'," said Mr Orton, 33.

They didn't. By 10.30am, the company director had seen enough and decided he needed to be at home with his family.

He said: "I'm coming back and the whole of Hull is flooded. It was half way up

the back of the Lexus. My mate who has got a building company brought a Jenny to pump the water out, which was three bricks up on the side of the house by then."

Like many in the city, the family went to bed that night wondering what they would wake up to the next morning. Their fears were realised.

Mr Orton said: "When we woke up it was over the skirting boards in the house and at that time we just gave up. The whole street was in the same mess."

The family and children Wayne Brookes, 18, and 11-year-old Lauren, were fortunate to find accommodation at the nearby Kingswood Hotel.

They have been there ever since, thankful that their insurance company is picking up the tab for the £49.95 it costs per night for a family room and the £7.50 each day for breakfast.

They return home each day to pick through their belongings, strewn across the lawn and bursting out of a skip on the drive.

Having bought the plot of land five years ago, they had the property built to their specifications, but now the Ortons have seen their dreams washed away.

Mr Orton said: "Every thing we have worked for is

gone. We have been told to gut it right up to the ceiling so we'll have to start from scratch again.

"We reckon we've lost about £25,000, but that's just the things we wrote down initially.

"I'm gutted. The thing was.

"We spent three months waiting for the sofa to come and then we only had it a month. Wayne has just left school and we had a prom party for him in the garden the Friday before. you just don't think how quickly things can change."

Kingswood was one of the worst hit areas in a ravaged city.

After four days an extensive pumping operation by the fire brigade had moved enough of the flood water into the River Hull for some aspects of normal life to return.

Mr Orton said: "On Friday

we'd just about finished the house.

morning they had a roadsweeper down here and they were cutting the grass. It was laughable."

Mr Orton and his neighbours suspended their clean-up operation mid-week to have a morale-boosting drink together at the local pub.

He said: "Everybody in this area is in the same boat so you have to cheer yourself up a bit. We went for a drink and had a joke about it, but then you come back and see it and it hits you again."

The family have no idea how long they will stay in the hotel or when they can come back to live in the house. Eating from a set menu is not straightforward

as Lauren has coeliac disease, making her allergic to gluten and wheat products.

They have been advised to look for somewhere to rent in the medium term as they try to rebuild their lives.

Mr Orton said: "It's heart wrenching. Your home is your castle, your pride and joy. I was proud to show people around my home but look at it now. It's embarrassing to see all your worldly possessions laid out on the lawn and people driving by to look. You take pride in providing a home for your family and then it's under water, it's gone. It affects your pride in yourself.

"We didn't want it to happen, we didn't want the water to come in. We just want to get back to normal."

simon.bristow@ypn.co.uk

Coping: Kevin Orton's home was badly flooded last week.

> "I'm gutted. The thing was, we'd just about finished the house."

Village heroes deserve praise for their actions

JOHN and Elaine Morgan were on a shopping trip to Hull when the rains came, but headed to what they thought would be the sanctuary of their home in Burton Pidsea.

As their journey east took in flooded village after flooded village they expected respite around every corner, not knowing that they too were already victims.

"We had no idea," said Mrs Morgan, 54, "We were feeling sorry for all the people in Bilton and Sproatley and then we got home at about half past-four and I just said, 'Oh my God' "

It seemed like the whole village was submerged.

As the evening wore on, the rains continued and the waters rose, they also realised they were on their own.

"No-one came to Burton Pidsea," said Mr Morgan, a former RAF fitter. "There were no police, no firemen, nobody from the council, and we couldn't get out of the village. We were trapped."

The couple and their grandson Lewis, like scores of others, would spend the next three nights on makeshift bedding in the village hall.

But not before they had witnessed collective acts of heroism that would make them proud of their small community.

Mr Morgan said: "There are pensioners bungalows on the other side of the street and there were old women just sitting there up to their knees in water.

"The lads in the village were going in and carrying them out one by one. They were brilliant. If it hadn't been for them we would have been burying people."

The 60-year-old described the nights in the village hall as "horrendous", but was again moved by the way his neighbours rallied round.

He said: "We were sharing the village hall with dogs, cats and parrots but people had donated mattresses and towels. Everybody was trying to make the best of it.

"The people who run the

village hall were amazing. They were coming in at 7.15 every morning to cook hot stew. I don't know what we'd have done without them."

Such is the strength of the village's resilience and powers of recovery that the Morgans are able to read a special flood edition copy of the July 2007 Burton Pidsea Newsletter as they sit in their garden on what little furniture they managed to salvage from their home in Glebelands.

This remarkable document, typed over two sides of a sheet of A4 paper, apologises for coming out late, offers thanks to all those who helped and announces the launch of a village disaster fund.

Along with a personal message of thanks from Doris Johnson, 100, for the cards and flowers she received on her birthday, is a range of advice on how to cope in the weeks ahead.

There are items on home security, how to restore flood-damaged photographs, and under the heading "Pets" the news that "Marion at the garage has the details of a lady in Preston who is willing to take in pets in the event of anything like this happening again"

For the Morgans the immediate future is uncertain.

They have been told it could be a year before the house is habitable again. Meanwhile they and Lewis, 14, are living in a small caravan and awning erected on their lawn.

Unlike many of their neighbours they at least have the comfort of home insurance to fall back on. The company is trying to send them a mobile home from Southend.

Less than a fortnight since disaster hit, there is still a sense of shock at how their lives were turned upside down in just one day.

Mr Morgan said: "I've been all over the world but I've never seen anything like this. But we know there are people worse off. At least we haven't died."

Home from home: John Morgan, 60, and his wife, Elaine, 56, are still smiling despite their home being wrecked after floods in Glebelands, Burton Pidsea.

After the downpour...

Washout: Firefighters struggle to reposition a pump during another downpour in Burstwick, above left, as residents carry belongings from their homes on Kingswood estate, Hull, above centre. Canoeists enjoy the floods in Beverley.

> "I have been all over the world but I have never seen anything at all like this."

(top left) Camping out – John Morgan and his wife Elaine of Burton Pidsea (see page 126).

(bottom right) Canoeists ride the floods in Beverley.

(bottom) Firefighters struggled to reposition a pump during another downpour in Burstwick.

10 SPECIAL PUBLICATION SATURDAY JULY 7 2007

www.yorkshirepost.co.uk

The Great Flood Opinion & Analysis

Knee deep: Francesca Granger carries her neighbour's daughter, Amy Jolly, three, as families are forced to leave their flooded homes in Bentley, near Doncaster, at the height of the floods.

Denis MacShane

Denis MacShane is MP for Rotherham

High time we looked closer to home when it comes to funding

THE most worrying aspect of this region's flooding tragedy is that it has been presented as an example of Yorkshire grit in the face of adversity.

It has not been understood as one of the greatest disasters caused by wayward nature that Britain has suffered in modern times.

The plain truth is that if any of the nation's elite of politicians, civil servants, business leaders and editors had suffered anything like the damage which has swamped Rotherham, Doncaster, Sheffield, Leeds, Hull and other areas, the news headlines would have reverberated for days.

Fellow MPs from areas where the rainfall was just good for gardens joked when they asked if Rotherham still existed. But it was no laughing matter. The television images of a man in Hull slowly being submerged as his leg was trapped – or the thought of a man being washed down the Wicker in Sheffield to be drowned in the heart of one of England's great cities – are unbearable.

Meadowhall, the global symbol of the shopping mall revolution, had to close down as it filled with water. Motorways and train routes were shut. We have all seen the pictures of hurricane damage in the United States or rivers bursting their banks in Europe, but never before have so many cities, towns and communities in Britain faced such a linked chain of calamities because of the awesome power of water.

Many people rose to the occasion. Firefighters donned lifesaving vests and rescue services showed a professionalism and sense of duty that did them much honour.

However, hard questions have to be asked. I frequently walk in the lovely country around the Ulley reservoir in Rotherham. I looked with horror at the yellow pipes snaking out of it as they desperately sucked water away to try and stop the pressure that threatened to turn the M1 into a scene from The Dambusters.

Yet the principles of reservoir engineering have not changed in decades, if not centuries. What is the quality of the cement and state of repair of all our reservoirs in the Peak District and those providing water to Yorkshire's cities?

Why are so many homes not properly insured? Do we need tougher rules, or more pressure, on the insurance companies to update policies? What direct help is government giving to flooded households and businesses? Do ninnyish planners force homes to be built in high-risk areas? Do we need an overhaul of our planning rules so that homes built on safer ground are given priority over the desire of people to guard unspoilt views?

The Government has appointed my fellow Rotherham MP, John Healey, as Floods Minister. He is one of the most respected Ministers in government. If anyone knows where the Treasury keeps its cash, it is Mr Healey.

Baptism of fire is perhaps the wrong metaphor to describe what John Healey is going through as he inspects the water damage done to Yorkshire, but this is a chance to show that a Hull home, a Sheffield road or a Rotherham business get the same attention as those in London when disaster strikes.

There are also more MPs from Yorkshire sitting in a Cabinet than at any time in British history. They know from first-hand experience the need for a unique act of solidarity to enable people to lead normal lives again.

Do we need a special Yorkshire committee of Cabinet Ministers to broach the walls of Whitehall to find the money to put the county back on its feet? After all, the Department for International Development has given more than £1bn to India in recent years and more than £1bn to management consultants at rich London firms to promote UK development policy in poor countries. Is it not time to spend a little more taxpayers' money a little closer to home at least until such time as every house is dry and re-decorated, every shop cleaned, every road, tunnel and drain repaired, every reservoir inspected and if necessary made good?

The great floods continue to make worldwide television and front page news. If they happened in America or France, states of emergencies would be declared, presidents would have visited and extra money been made available for the rebuilding operation.

Back home, we put the kettle on and make everyone a nice cup of tea. This typical Britain-can-take-it response is something to be proud of. But we are one nation and it is time that the nation, and its leaders, understood the damage Yorkshire has suffered – and the urgent need for leadership and resources to help put things right.

Morning delivery: Food is handed out to residents by boat as Doncaster Council workers tour houses in Toll Bar, near Doncaster.

Letters to the Editor

From: Malcolm Marsh, Towers Lane, Crofton, Wakefield.

I NOTE that the Bishop of Liverpool, among other church leaders, has declared that the recent floods are "God's judgment on recent pro-gay legislation".

Perhaps the good bishop (Yorkshire Post, July 3) would put his deep thinking to the plight of hundreds of thousands of people across Africa and ask why where the Christian churches are extremely anti-gay, they have been visited by greater devastation in the form of drought and consequent famine.

I am a practising and communicant Christian, and find no difficulty in understanding why the congregations are small and diminishing when a high ranking member of the Church of England can use his high office to utter such drivel.

From: W Ruddlesdin, Upper Hoyland Road, Hoyland, Barnsley.

IF the Bishops of Carlisle and Liverpool blame the floods in our area on God, why has no Divine Intervention been made in the area surrounding his birth?

From the Stern gangs of the 1940s to the present day violence of various religious factions, surely some miracle would occur.

From: Bill Marsh, Low Green, Copmanthorpe, York.

I TRUST that Gordon Brown will re-direct some of the massive funds he has committed for overseas aid to look after our own in Hull and South Yorkshire? The people who created the funds in the first place through direct and indirect taxation surely must have first call on the money.

From: Geraldine Bristow, Hope Street, Staincross, Barnsley.

WHAT a logical explanation to the cause of the recent floods from Dennis Wilcock (Yorkshire Post, June 30). It makes perfect sense as to why water isn't being absorbed into an already sodden ground.

As for the clearing of ditches and dykes, they are full of plastic bottles and discarded litter. Perhaps this is a job for the unemployed of the country, a way in which they can earn their benefit, similar to that of a child in the "good old days" when pocket money was a reward in return for small tasks being done.

In that way, we wouldn't have to see them daily sitting outside public houses for most of the afternoon while we have been hard at it in a stuffy office working for a living.

From: Della Petch, Burdale Close, Driffield, East Yorkshire.

WITHIN three months of the devastating floods in central Europe in 2002, the European Commission set up the "Solidarity Fund" to be used to restore vital infrastructure and equipment after natural disasters.

The first use of this fund freed up £444 million for Germany, £134 million for Austria, £129 million for the Czech Republic and £31 million for France.

Remarkably, the Czech Republic was not even a full member of the EU at the time – not joining until 2004. Since 2002, the fund has provided hundreds of millions of Euros for flood repair in Italy, Spain, Estonia, Portugal, Austria, and elsewhere.

The flood hit counties in England have received nothing to date. We deserve better than this. We must have our own Parliament and our own national representatives, who will put our country first and are answerable to us, the people; not one infested with self serving rats, who care only about what they can do for their Scottish master and who, like Hull's MP John Prescott, are all too ready to jump the sinking ship when the effluent closes in on them.

From: R Hughes, Muston Road, Filey.

I READ with increasing concern your article about flooding problems in Filey (Yorkshire Post, July 3). I was flooded in 2002 and spent seven months out of my home.

Last week I was only just in time to prevent sewage feeding back into my shower and toilet. Water was bubbling into the shower tray again during the recent heavy thunder rain.

I have reported this to the water company. If this is happening now, what is likely to happen in Filey if 300 more houses are built on Muston Road? When is the planning committee going to accept the advice of the consultants and do no more development in this area until the problem of the sewers has been dealt with?

I have spent several hundred pounds since 2002 in an attempt to make my home less vulnerable. I accepted with gratitude the sand bags provided because we would be "at risk" and have spent this last week or so blocking and unblocking air bricks, and now they are inside as well – a new addition to the downstairs toilet. We keep being told of plans and work starting "soon" and still nothing happens. I despair.

From: R Raine, Narrow Lane, Harden, Bingley.

THE deafening silence and inactivity of the Government is in complete contrast to the wonderful actions of the rescue and support services saving hundreds of lives and property in the recent floods. It is the Government's responsibility to ensure adequate flood defences and anticipate the results of climate change. No excuses! We demand – not ask – that 100 per cent compensation is paid to all those who have suffered loss throughout the country through this neglect.

"MPs joked when asking if Rotherham still existed ... It was no laughing matter."

www.yorkshirepost.co.uk

SPECIAL PUBLICATION SATURDAY JULY 7 2007   **11**

The Great Flood The Ministers' response

Priority must be to help victims

Environment Secretary **Hilary Benn** and Communities Secretary **Hazel Blears** respond to critics who say the Government has been slow to respond to the crisis.

THE people of Yorkshire have had their lives turned upside down by the recent floods. Many people will be living with disruption for months to come. The devastating effect on lives is hard to imagine for anyone who has not been through this experience.

We have both been to visit communities affected by the flooding, including Sheffield, Bentley and Toll Bar. We have witnessed the very trying conditions, and heard first-hand from those affected.

Local people told us about their experiences – some were angry and many were distressed. And they had understandable fears, not just about the immediate future but about what events like this mean for the long-term security of their homes and communities.

The priority now is to help communities to recover as quickly as possible. Local Government Minister John Healey is leading the cross-Government recovery effort. He has already met Ministers and officials. He has also visited some of the places affected to see the situation on the ground, in particular Hull, which has been very badly affected.

Local leaders have been a tower of strength for local communities, taking immediate steps to help people to cope. We will make sure that central Government gives them the vital support they need now.

Already, we have been in contact with 12 local authorities and given advice on how they can apply for emergency financial support. Councils can use these funds to help pay for the costs of immediate support to safeguard life and property, and other urgent action they need to take to help pick up the pieces in the weeks to come.

The insurance companies have put on extra staff to deal with claims, but there's a big problem of householders with no insurance.

Work and Pensions Secretary Peter Hain has pledged support for householders on low incomes who are desperately worried about the costs of flood damage to their homes. Crisis loans can help people struggling to pay for essential items, and Jobcentre Plus staff are present at evacuation centres to make sure people know how to apply. There are also non-repayable Community Care Grants available to some. We're making sure that the process for dealing with applications is as swift as possible.

Yorkshire Forward is working with the Government and local authorities to put in place business support. A £1m small business recovery scheme has been launched. Already, they have begun contacting companies to discuss how best to deliver the support they need.

The Government is working with the insurance industry, through the Association of British

Insurers, and there are arrangements in place to ensure that insurance continues to be available for as many customers as possible.

In the longer term, it is essential that we keep a close watch on the relationship between development and flood risk. Urban planning has a significant role to play. There are few areas which have no risk of flooding at all, and we have built on areas of risk throughout history for some sound social and economic reasons.

The key thing is to manage risk and ensure not only that new buildings are safe, but that they don't increase flood risk to others. The Environment Agency has to be consulted on council plans for new housing. Since October last year, it has to be consulted on planning applications where flood risk is an issue.

It's certainly clear that flood resilience measures for individual properties will play an increasingly important role as our climate changes.

We recently launched a pilot scheme to test the feasibility of grants for helping people install measures in their homes to reduce flood risk.

Measures include using temporary door-guards and waterproof render to stop water getting into the home, and wake resistant walls and floors – or raised electricity points to minimise damage inside the home– if water does get in.

The Environment Agency's Floodline remains an important source of information about flood risk and we would encourage everyone to check whether they are in an at-risk area and to use the Floodline when extreme weather warnings are given. The telephone number is 08459 881188.

The Agency also publishes flood warnings on its website.

We wish we could give people the assurance that this won't happen again. We can't do that, because it is not as simple as spending more money. On Monday, we announced an increase in our spending on flood defences from the record level of £600m this year to £800m by 2011.

But exceptional flooding like this can happen even where there are defences in place - indeed many of the places flooded in recent weeks do have existing defences.

These defences didn't fail, they were simply overwhelmed by the extraordinary volume of water falling in a very short time.

Over the last few days, we have witnessed the devastating impact of floods on communities and sympathise with all those who have suffered damage and distress.

We thank the many who have responded to these events locally, including the emergency services, local authorities and voluntary organisations.

Scene of devastation: The sheer scale of the flooding near Rotherham left homes, businesses, roads, railways and farmland under water.

Rescue services are left stunned

Kate O'Hara

EVEN those who spend their lives dealing with emergency situations were shocked at how quickly the waters rose – and the devastation brought in their wake.

Firefighters in West Yorkshire, South Yorkshire and Humberside were some of the first on the scene in the areas ravaged by floods, and were amazed by the scenes they were met with.

David Gardiner, 51, Calderdale District Manager, had been at the force's headquarters in Birkinshaw on the afternoon of Monday June 25 when he was told about the floods and made his way to South Elmsall to co-ordinate the area's flood operation.

"Even the fire station was flooded, it was unbelievable," he said. "It was like there was a raging torrent of water rushing past us.

"There wasn't even a road there anymore at all – it was just a fast-flowing river.

"I had never, ever seen anything like it in my life."

A priority was to try to grab hold of the heavy debris which was being quickly carried along by the waters and smashing into property.

"We had beer barrels, beds and all sorts of things floating past at high speed.

"There was even a gas cylinder which had been ripped clean out of a caravan which was hissing gas – posing a major explosive hazard," said Mr Gardiner.

"I've been in the fire service for 29 and a half years and I've never seen anything like it before.

"There was little we could do at that point apart from rescue people. We couldn't start pumping out because the water was still rising – and quickly.

"Things got even worse as the night went on and in the early hours of the morning.

"No amount of experience could prepare you for the scenes of that night – and the results have been devastating."

Firefighters from as far away as Devon came to South Yorkshire to help.

Mark Smitherman, Chief Fire Officer for South Yorkshire Fire and Rescue, described the events of the last week as a "testing time" for staff.

They were called to help in rescues and evacuations, as well as some serious fires.

"Judging by the testimonials I've already received from the public, I am not the only one who wants to thank our firefighters, control room operators and all other staff for their tireless dedication.

"I would also like to extend our thanks to colleagues in other fire and rescue services across the country," he said.

Mr Smitherman said fire crews were now helping the people of Toll Bar to revisit their homes, and the service would help with the clean-up operation for as long as they were needed.

yorkshirepost.co.uk
Please sign our petition and help us to force the Government to help the flood-hit communities across Yorkshire. You can send us your comments and view a complete archive of our floods coverage, including reports on video, at www.yorkshirepost.co.uk/flooding

FLOODING TIMELINE

- **Monday, June 25:** Torrential downpours hit Yorkshire as parts of the region are paralysed by the heaviest rainfall in 50 years.
- Thousands of people evacuated from Leeds, Hull, Barnsley, Rotherham and Sheffield.
- River Don and River Aire burst their banks. 85,000 homes left without power.
- Three people lose their lives.
- Hundreds trapped at Ridgnaide Lane, Sheffield and have to be rescued by RAF helicopters.
- Major transport disruption on roads and railway.

- **Tuesday, June 26:** Demands for extra financial help headed aside by Environment Secretary David Miliband.
- Eight thousand insurance claims received in 24 hours.
- Five crews battle to stop Ulley reservoir near Rotherham from bursting its banks and destroying villages. M1 closed.
- **Thursday, June 28:** Homes and businesses hit in Pickering, North Yorkshire.
- Leeds Council vows to put pressure on Defra to resurrect £100m flood defence scheme shelved for three years.
- **Wednesday, June 27:** Environment Agency continues building defences in Sheffield unlikely to start for at least three years.

- Householders in Sheffield face planned power cuts as supply affected.
- Heavy duty pumps brought in for East Yorkshire.
- Residents from Bentley, Hexthorpe, Arksey and Absholm, South Yorkshire out of their homes.
- Private security guards drafted in to help police protect communities abandoned in Sheffield floods.
- **Friday June 29:** Prince Charles (below) visits Catcliffe, near Rotherham, and vows to used Royal influence to help Sheffield Forgemasters get back on its feet.
- Association of British Insurers predicts cost of damage will top £1bn.
- Massive rescue effort to protect flood-hit areas with more rain forecast.

- **Sunday, July 1:** Large parts of Bentley and Toll Bar, near Doncaster still under water.
- **Monday, July 2:** Hilary Benn (below right) reveals Government will increase flood defence budget from £600m a year to £800m but refuses to give in to demands for extra financial help for flood-hit areas.
- Frustrated residents in Toll Bar and Bentley near Doncaster told it may be days before they return home to look at the damage to their houses.
- **Tuesday, July 3:** 35,000 residents now homeless by the devastating floods in Hull alone – almost 40,000 people in Yorkshire.
- Carl Minns, leader of Hull Council, calls for urgent Government support after revealing the city is worst-hit place in the country.

- **Sunday, July 1:** City Council allocates £10m crisis fund.
- **Wednesday, July 4:** Prince Charles returns to South Yorkshire to visit flood victims in Toll Bar.
- The Prince of Wales climbs into a small boat to get a close-up look at the devastation.

Graphic: Graeme Bandeira

> "We wish we could give people assurances this won't happen again ... We can't."

12 SPECIAL PUBLICATION SATURDAY JULY 7 2007 www.yorkshirepost.co.uk

The Great Flood The impact

HOW YORKSHIRE'S WORST WEATHER FOR SEVEN YEARS UNFOLDED

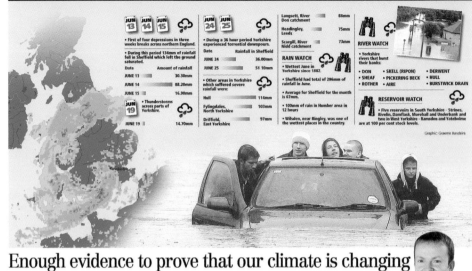

JUN 13 JUN 14 JUN 15
- First of four depressions in three weeks breaks across northern England.
- During this period 134mm of rainfall fell in Sheffield which left the ground saturated.

Date	Amount of rainfall
JUNE 13	30.30mm
JUNE 14	88.20mm
JUNE 15	16.90mm

JUN 19
- Thunderstorms across parts of Yorkshire.

JUNE 19	14.70mm

JUN 24 JUN 25
- During a 36 hour period Yorkshire experienced torrential downpours.

Date	Rainfall in Sheffield
JUNE 24	36.00mm
JUNE 25	51 10mm

- Other areas in Yorkshire which suffered severe rainfall were:

Hull	114mm
Fylingdales, North Yorkshire	103mm
Driffield, East Yorkshire	97mm

Langsett, River Don catchment		88mm
Headingley, Leeds		75mm
Scargill, River Nidd catchment		73mm

RAIN WATCH
- Wettest June in Yorkshire since 1882.
- Sheffield had total of 286mm of rainfall in June.
- Average for Sheffield for the month is 67mm.
- 100mm of rain in Humber area in 12 hours
- Wilsden, near Bingley, was one of the wettest places in the country.

RIVER WATCH
- Yorkshire rivers that burst their banks:
- DON
- SHEAF
- ROTHER
- SKELL (RIPON)
- PICKERING BECK
- AIRE
- DERWENT
- HULL
- BURSTWICK DRAIN

RESERVOIR WATCH
- Five reservoirs in South Yorkshire – Strines, Rivelin, Damflask, Morehall and Underbank and two in West Yorkshire – Ramsden and Yateholme are at 100 per cent stock levels.

Graphic: Graeme Bandeira

Enough evidence to prove that our climate is changing

THE first 10 days of June were warm and dry giving little indication of the deluge to come.

Then, on June 13, the first of four weather depressions arrived, acting as a catalyst for the devastating floods.

Three days of heavy rainfall left much of Yorkshire saturated, so when the torrential downpours of June 24 and 25 occurred, the water had nowhere to go – turning roads and paths into rivers.

In Hull and much of East Yorkshire, the flooding was not caused by rivers spilling their banks, or failing flood defences, but by rainwater unable to escape through overflowing drains, or into flat ground that was already drenched from the earlier heavy rains.

In Sheffield, record-breaking rainfall combined with steeper land that sent water rushing into nearby rivers, proved catastrophic.

BBC weather expert Paul Hudson believes the recent floods were more severe than those that struck seven years ago.

The floods of autumn 2000 also followed a wet summer and Mr Hudson warned there could be more in store now.

"The worry is that if we don't get much dry weather and there is a wet autumn then we could be facing more flooding."

He is in little doubt that we are witnessing climate change.

"In the last 12 months or so we have seen the hottest July ever recorded, autumn was also the warmest ever on record, April 2007 was also the warmest ever recorded and June is now the wettest.

"All these records have been broken and climate scientists tell us that it's going to get warmer and wetter. I believe there is enough evidence just here in Yorkshire to show that we are living through a period of climate change," he said.

"Twenty or 30 years ago people were at risk of being flooded if they lived near a river, but now anybody can be at risk and we are in this together."

Warning: Paul Hudson believes our climate is changing.

We must be wary of record figures

Philip Eden is Vice President of the Royal Meteorological Society Here he outlines the cause of the floods and why there may be more bad weather on the way

THE first signs that this summer might be rather out of the ordinary appeared in early spring. Throughout eight long weeks there was little or no rain over large parts of the UK, and April was the warmest and one of the driest ever recorded.

It all seems such a long time ago now. Extended spring droughts are often followed by poor summers, and there is a reason for this.

When a particular weather pattern becomes stuck over western Europe for several weeks in spring, there is a well-known tendency for it to shift westwards by early summer: Thus the high pressure system which had dominated March and April slipped away into mid-Atlantic by the second week of May, and this allowed Atlantic depressions to travel round the top of the "high", then to plunge southeastwards towards the British Isles.

Apart from a ten-day break at the beginning of June, this sequence of depressions has continued over since.

June 2007 was certainly an exceptional month, and local rainfall records were broken in the Birmingham, Nottingham, and Lincoln areas, as well as over much of Yorkshire. However, rainfall totals varied widely from one part of the country to another.

Northern Scotland had a very dry month, while many parts of southern England reported only small excesses.

Averaged over England and Wales it turned out to be the wettest June since 1860, just pipping 1997 which was the wettest of the last century. There were quite large variations within Yorkshire's boundaries, too.

The devastating floods which affected many parts of Yorkshire, but especially Sheffield, the Don valley and Hull from June 20 onwards were the result of a double whammy.

It is hardly ever mentioned, but most parts of Yorkshire actually had more rainfall during the earlier downpour, between June 13 and 15, when the resultant flooding that the quite appreciably less severe and less widespread.

But, by the time the second downpour arrived, the water table was very high, the flood-plains were sodden, river levels remained very high, and there was simply nowhere for the billions of gallons of additional water to go.

One striking aspect of June's weather was the fact that the mean monthly temperature ended up over a degree above the average for the standard reference period 1971-2000, indicating that the underlying warming trend is identifiable even during our dullest and wettest months.

We have notoriously fallible memories when it comes to newsworthy weather events, but here in the UK our records of rainfall and temperature are second to none, providing us with a descriptive and statistical background to the British climate extending back to the late-17th century.

However, statistics can be easily mis-used. We should guard against labelling events as "a new record" or "unprecedented", because then the people who pay to keep our infrastructure running have a ready-made excuse for failure: "It's never happened before so how could we be expected to plan for it?"

June may have been the wettest month on record at Weston Park in Sheffield, but more rain fell in Leeds in June 1982, while a similar amount fell in Longdendale, west of Sheffield, in July 1973.

On both occasions there was severe, widespread, and long-lasting flooding in different parts of Yorkshire. The county is also particularly prone to short-lived flash flooding following violent thunderstorms: June 2005 in Helmsley, May 1989 in Halifax, the western suburbs of Bradford in August 1956, and Ilkley in July 1900 all spring to mind.

No one should be allowed to escape from low pressure anchored near southwestern Britain in late-June has now given way to low pressure to the north of Scotland. So there have been changes.

My expectation is that August will be appreciably drier and warmer, without quite being the settled holiday month that most people are hoping for. since then low pressure "never happened before" line. More to the point, it will happen again. When our summer weather pattern gets stuck, it sometimes takes until late-August or early-September – when the declining heat energy from the sun begins to exert an influence – before there is a major change.

But I don't believe we have become stuck in such a rut. It is easy to forget that the first ten days of June were dry and settled with high pressure in charge, and

yorkshirepost.co.uk
What do you think? Visit our website and have 'Your Say'

GIVE YOUR SUPPORT

- **South Yorkshire flood fund:** Run by South Yorkshire Community Foundation – to donate visit www.justgiving.com/south yorkshirefloodrelief or pay cash into Yorkshire Bank through sort code 05-08-03, account number 21890703.

- **Sheffield Council:** To make a donation send cheque, made payable to Sheffield Council's Lord Mayor's Charity Flood Fund, to The Lord Mayor's Office, Town Hall, Sheffield, S1 2HH.

- **Hallam FM flood victim support appeal:** To donate to this appeal, make your cheque payable to South Yorkshire Flood Victim Support Appeal, and pay it in at any branch of the Yorkshire Bank.

- **Hull Flood Fund:** A Hull Flood Fund has been set up to help the most vulnerable people in the city. Donations can be made at any branch of Natwest bank in Hull and the East Riding.

- **Wakefield's Mayor, Clir Allan Garbutt, has launched a flood relief fund:** Cheques made payable to Wakefield MDC can be sent to Cash Office, Chantry House, 123 Kirkgate, Wakefield WF1 1ZS. Please indicate that the cheque is intended for flood relief. Cash donations can be made in person at Chantry House. Please do not send cash through the post.

Pictures: Chris Lawton, Terry Carrott, Simon Hulme, Gary Longbottom, Jim Moran, Bruce Rollinson, Tony Bartholomew, Sean Spencer, John Jones, Ross Parry Agency and Press Association.

Photographs taken by Yorkshire Post photographers can be purchased from Photo Sales on 0113 238 8360 or www.photostoday.co.uk

Under water: Council workers check houses in Bentley near Doncaster, South Yorkshire after flood waters swept through the streets. Emergency co-ordinators worked tirelessly to ensure residents were evacuated from areas devastated by the floods.

"This is a period of climate change... Anybody can be at risk, we are in it together"

Under water:
Council workers checked houses in Bentley near Doncaster, South Yorkshire after flood waters swept through the streets. Emergency co-ordinators worked tirelessly to ensure residents were evacuated from areas devastated by the floods.

June 15. Firemen rescued John Ward and Barnaby Dove from their property off the A656 at Allerton Bywater after flooding closed the road. *Picture: Bruce Rollinson.*

June 25: The Fire Brigade checked houses in Doncaster Road, Darfield Bridge, Barnsley after the level of the River Dearne rose overnight flooding the area.
Picture Bruce Rollinson.

Another picture of the flooding off Doncaster Road, Darfield Bridge, Barnsley on June 25. *Picture Bruce Rollinson*

Homes in Darfield
swamped after the River
Deaner burst its banks.

Swift and very dangerous, the swollen River Dearne in Darfield.

Fire fighters pass an abandoned car on Cliffe Road off Doncaster Road, Darfield Bridge.
Picture Bruce Rollinson

Water swirled past
houses in Darfield.
*Picture Bruce
Rollinson*

June 25. A man rescued belongings from a caravan at Willowbridge Caravan site, as the waters of the adjacent River Don continue to rise.
Picture Bruce Rollinson

A couple forced to leave their house in Petersgate, Scawthorpe, Doncaster. *Picture Bruce Rollinson*

A boy on his bike in the flood waters in Petersgate, Scawthorpe, Doncaster. *Picture Bruce Rollinson*

Some necessities rescued from his home, a householder in Jossey Avenue, Scawthorpe, Doncaster, waded through the lake that now stretched beyond his front door. *Picture Bruce Rollinson.*

June 16. Flooding on the Boroughbridge Road at Ripon provided a frightening spectacle. *Picture: Bruce Rollinson*

A driver is stranded on Northern Street, off Wellington Street, Leeds.

(right) James Halliwell tried to tape the French doors to keep flood waters out of his brother's house in Liversedge.

Nice weather for ducks, but disastrous for householders in Weavergate, Liversedge. *Picture: Jim Moran*

Gardens in Weavergate, Liversedge, were turned into swimming pools, but no-one would want to swim in this flood water.

Picture: Jim Moran

Also in Westgate, Wakefield, a boy launched himself into the flood on his bicycle, hoping the water wouldn't slow his momentum and bring him off with a splash. *Picture Gary Longbottom*

A barber clambered over sandbags protecting his property from the flooding in Westgate, Wakefield.

No place for a pedestrian as
the main street in Darton,
near Barnsley, was engulfed
by the swollen River Dearne.
Picture Gary Longbottom

Nothing for it but to paddle barefoot to the hairdressers when the Dearne at
Darton burst its banks. *Picture Gary Longbottom*

In a car park at Darton, a car submerged by the flood. *Picture Gary Longbottom.*

The day when crossing Darton's main street was like fording a stream in spate.

Worrying times for Janet Ashby of Low Barugh near Barnsley, ankle deep in flood water on her patio as a neighbour stacked sand bags against the door of her house when the flooding River Dearne drowned the garden.

Picture Gary Longbottom

When the beer garden at the Millers Inn, Low Barugh near Barnsley, was turned into a water garden. Landlord Wayne Stephenson, up to his knees in the flood water.
Picture Gary Longbottom

4.4 m
14'6"

Benches from the
Millers Inn were swept
away by the torrent.
*Picture Gary
Longbottom.*

Wayne Stephenson (right) helped locals negotiate fast-flowing flood waters. *Picture Gary Longbottom*

Cattle gathered on the high ground in fields off the A637 swamped by the River Dearne. *Picture Gary Longbottom*

A van driver checked the water level as he carefully negotiated a flooded road through the middle of Normanby village near Pickering. *Picture Gary Longbottom.*

On the same stretch of road, a driver hoped for the best. Having started, when the water is this deep you just have to keep going and hope to reach dry land before the engine conks out. *Picture Gary Longbottom*

Roger Hudson of Sinnington near Pickering inspected a massive tree stump deposited by the flooded River Seven.
Picture Gary Longbottom

The awful aftermath. Neighbours helped clear Bridge Cottage, the home of Christine Slowther of Sinnington, after the River Seven flooded the house late at night on June 25. *Picture Gary Longbottom*

Walking the dog - or swimming the dog? A resident of Pickering took her pet for an airing through the flooded town.
Picture Gary Longbottom

When benches, carefully positioned to give a pleasant view of the stream, become part of the stream. These were engulfed by the swollen Pickering Beck which flooded the town. *Picture Gary Longbottom.*

Oops! A very awkward moment, almost ending in an unscheduled bath, in Pickering's flooded Market Place. *Picture Gary Longbottom*

It's all right for some... a young man keeps his feet dry while a young lady gets hers very wet in a flooded Pickering street.

The Five Weirs Walk blocked on June 25 with debris on the banks of the Don near Meadow Hall Road, Sheffield.
Picture Chris Lawton

When "Beck Isle" Museum in Pickering lived up to its name. *Picture Gary Longbottom*

Traffic lights bent by the flood water in Brightside Lane, Sheffield. *Picture Chris Lawton.*

After the flood: damaged cars in Brightside Lane, Sheffield. *Picture Chris Lawton.*

July 1. Two wheels are better than one… as pumping goes on in Tollbar, near Doncaster. *Picture Chris Lawton*

It's an ill wind… home bound security worker Abdal Mousa of Pitsmoor, Sheffield, with two fish found in Brightside Lane, Sheffield. He said he was going to eat them. *Picture Chris Lawton.*

Clear-up after the flood at Meadowhall Shopping Centre, Sheffield. *Picture Chris Lawton*

Sand bags for the doors
of Our Lady of Perpetual
Help Catholic Church,
High Street, Bentley.
Picture Chris Lawton

Sand bags hold back water in Chapel Street, Bentley. *Picture Chris Lawton*

The pump which moved flood water over a mile away from Bentley High Street, Doncaster. *Picture Chris Lawton*

Sand bags in
Church Street,
Bentley. *Picture Chris
Lawton.*

Locals watch the flood waters from the safety of a disused railway bridge in the centre of Catcliffe, Rotherham. *Picture Chris Lawton*

Flood waters
in Catcliffe,
Rotherham.
*Picture Chris
Lawton*

June 25. A caravan floated down the main road in Catcliffe, Rotherham.
Picture Chris Lawton.

Road sign in the main road in Catcliffe, Rotherham, more useful to sailors than motorists. *Picture Chris Lawton*

No calls from here for a while...a phone box in
Catcliffe. *Picture Chris Lawton*

One way to cross the flood water in Sprotbrough Road, Sprotbrough, Doncaster. *Picture Chris Lawton*

Young people walk through the flood water in Strotbough Road, Sprotbrough. *Picture Chris Lawton*

Farmer John Dickinson of Manor
Farm, Scaftworth, Bawtry near
Doncaster, in one of his fields flooded
when the River Idle burst its banks
two weeks earlier, killing off feed for
his 250 Jersey cattle.
Picture Chris Lawton.

John Emmerson in his flooded bathroom with his carp he saved by putting it in the bath before the flood at Toll Bar, Doncaster. *Picture Chris Lawton*

Police cross the A19 by boat as pumping goes on in Toll Bar. *Picture Chris Lawton*

"We'll be Back". Graham Parker sprays his defiant message on the front of his Motorist Discount shop on the A19 Askern Road in Toll Bar. *Picture Chris Lawton*

Millie Nettleton, eight, waded through the water on Cliff Road, Darfield. She had just visited her grandparents house which was flooded out.

Cheryl Guest sat outside her home at Millbeck Gardens, Collingham, with all the ground-floor furniture ruined by the floods.

The damage caused to Ulley Dam after the floods of Monday, June 25.

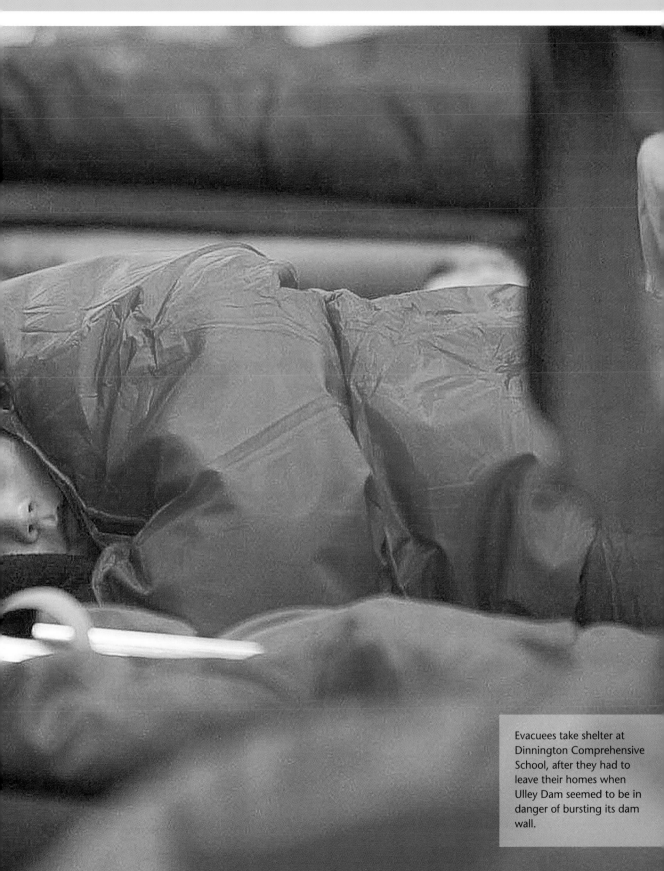

Evacuees take shelter at Dinnington Comprehensive School, after they had to leave their homes when Ulley Dam seemed to be in danger of bursting its dam wall.

Cars at a car dealer are submerged, after the floods at Toll Bar, Doncaster.

Flood misery. Collecting a duvet from a flooded home on Dunhill Crescent, Wykebeck, Leeds.

Post master John Jackson stands outside his flooded shop at Toll Bar, Doncaster.

Despair and uncertainty - refugees fled the flooded Kingswood estate in north Hull. *Picture: Terry Carrott*

Helping hands in a time of need on the Kingswood estate.
Picture: Terry Carrott

Floods threatened houses alongside the Westwood in York Road, Beverley. *Picture: Terry Carrott*

A cyclist made his way through deep flood water in Pasture Terrace, Beverley.
Picture: Terry Carrott

A picture of good spirits in adversity: a nurse cheered up an elderly lady as she joined 300 others in Hull City Hall after being evacuated from the floods. *Picture: Terry Carrott*

The sheer horror of it: Kevin Orton with furniture and belongings from his flooded home on Knightley Way, Kingswood Estate, Hull. *Picture: Terry Carrott*

Coping as best they could: John Morgan and his wife, Elaine, outside their home after it had been wrecked by the floods in Glebelands Burton Pidsea, East Yorkshire. They had to move into a tent on the lawn. *Picture: Terry Carrott*

GERVASE PHINN: SCHOOLS THAT FAIL OUR CHILDREN – FOCUS, PAGE 11

Yorkshire's National Newspaper

YORKSHIRE POST

45p   www.yorkshirepost.co.uk   TUESDAY JUNE 26 2007

RAF answer SOS to airlift terrified office workers

Boy, 13, swept to his death in park tragedy

Man dies trapped in manhole by rising waters

Hundreds stranded as raging storm floods claim two lives

Emergency: A rescue helicopter hovers over a factory in Sheffield where 20 people were rescued from rising floodwater.

Picture: Barry Batchelor/PA

Rob Preece, Kate O'Hara, Alexandra Wood and Tom Smithard

A MASSIVE airlift was under way in South Yorkshire last night to rescue scores of trapped people after a day of torrential rain and flooding claimed two lives.

With no signs of any let-up in the weather, police searching for a 13-year-old boy swept away in the River Sheaf in Sheffield's Millhouses Park reported last night that his body had been found.

In Sheffield, RAF search and rescue helicopters were used to airlift hundreds of trapped office workers to safety after the River Don burst its banks, sending a raging torrent through the city's industrial heartland. Terrified staff were left trapped on upper floors pleading for help, as buildings collapsed around them.

Apart from the airlift, many of the trapped workers were carried to safety by boats.

Elsewhere, as the region was paralysed by the heaviest rainfall in 50 years, a man in Hull died after he was trapped in a drain by rising waters.

Mike Barnett, 28, died after becoming trapped in a manhole, despite a desperate four-hour rescue operation to save his life.

He was trying to clear a large drain of debris in Astral Close, Hessle, near Hull, when his foot got caught in the grating.

Across the region, major roads remained gridlocked for hours, parts of the M1, A1, M62 and A63 being completely submerged. A series of railway stations, including Sheffield and Leeds, were

Flooding emergency: Above, fire service boats rescue people trapped in the Brightside area of Sheffield. Right, Hull victim Mike Barnett died in a manhole trap.

Main picture: Simon Hulme

closed and hundreds of bus services were cancelled.

Hundreds of people were evacuated from cities, towns and villages across Yorkshire. More rivers were expected to burst their banks overnight and people were told not to attempt to go to work today unless it was necessary.

Dozens were evacuated from Leeds city centre to two emergency shelters after the River Aire broke its banks.

Those stranded in Sheffield city centre, including the railway station and its surrounding area, were told to make their way to the Winter Gardens where they would be directed to safety.

A further 100 people were stranded at the Meadowhall shopping centre with no power or means of exit. Centre director Mohammed Dajani described the Oasis restaurant area as "a lake".

After a day of rescues that saw all of Yorkshire's fire services stretched to breaking point, the RAF had to send a series of helicopters to Sheffield to airlift people trapped on the roofs of industrial units on Brightside Lane, in the Lower Don Valley.

Many motorists trapped on the road also had to climb on top of

their cars to escape the rising floodwater.

A series of buildings in Brightside Lane, in the Attercliffe area of the city, were in danger of collapsing. Phil Davies, who was stuck on the upper floors of an office building, said it had become a "tributary of the River Don".

He said: "Retaining walls are collapsing, several have come down, and some of these walls are 100 years old. There are car bonnets submerged. There's no way of getting out. It's like a floodplain."

Another witness said the water had risen 3ft to 4ft in the space of 10 minutes after the River Don burst its banks.

A further 300 people were trapped on the first floor of the nearby Royal Mail distribution centre in Sheffield, without power.

Also in Sheffield last night, 300 people were taken from their homes in the Winn Garden estate in the Middlewood area and set up camp in two local schools.

Last night Sheffield Brightside MP David Blunkett said: "The armed services are doing a first class job. Briefings are being co-ordinated for Ministers and I will be seeking substantial financial Government help for those affected.

"The emergency services deserve great praise and my heart goes out to the people of Sheffield who have been affected. I will do everything possible to secure additional assistance as it is required."

In the Hull tragedy, Geoffrey Claxton, 76, who was employed victim Mike Barnett at the family-run fish importing business, said he had been working to clear the drain in Astral Close himself when the tragedy began at about 11am.

He said: "I was trying to get the detritus from the grid. I was in there with my chest waders and I was starting to get a bit shaky. He came over and said: 'Get yourself out, there's nothing you can do.' He got hold of me and he pulled me out."

Mr Claxton said he went back into the house for a shower and to warm up. When he returned,

Continued on Page 4

WORST FLOODING FOR FIFTY YEARS CRIPPLES CITIES – SEE PAGES 4, 5, 6 & 7

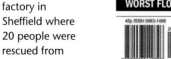

45p ISSN 0963-1496

Business	Section B	Letters to the Editor	12		
Classified	17,18	Local News	8		
Comment	12	Public Sector			
Family Notices	10	Appointments	16,17		
Focus	11	Sport	19-22		
News	2-7,9,10	TV and Radio	14		
UK & World News	15				

Weather   Dry with sunny intervals.
Full forecast: Back Page

0113 243 2701

News   8796
yp.newsdesk@ypn.co.uk
Sport   8473
yp.sport@ypn.co.uk
Business   8959
business.post@ypn.co.uk
Features   8952
yp.features@ypn.co.uk

6 YORKSHIRE POST TUESDAY JUNE 26 2007 www.yorkshirepost.co.uk

The floods

FOR INFORMATION AND HELP
National Rail Inquiries: 08457 484950
Floodline: 0845 988 1188
AA traffic and weather information line: 09003 401 100

999 calls come in at one a minute

Downpour overcomes sandbag defences

NORTH YORKSHIRE
Brian Dooks

SCHOOLS and homes were flooded and roads were left impassable as up to three inches of rain fell in North Yorkshire in 24 hours.

At one stage North Yorkshire Fire and Rescue Service said it was receiving an unprecedented number of 999 calls – reaching one every minute.

It also responded to requests for help from the Humberside and West Yorkshire Fire Services. A high-volume pump from Harrogate was sent to deal with a serious flooding incident in Castleford

The Fire Service appealed to the public to use the 999 system rather than try to telephone individual fire stations so calls could be prioritised.

Retained firefighters from Summerbridge, near Harrogate, were called to the primary school in the village where they are based after surface water flowing down the main street began over

flowing into the school, which is on a lower level.

The firefighters attempted to build a sandbag wall to keep the worst of the water out of the school, but teaching staff were forced to send home the 33 pupils.

With the Meteorological Office issuing a severe

The fire service appealed to the public to use the 999 system so calls could be prioritised

weather warning that all areas would receive an inch of rain with up to three inches in places, the Fire Service urged anyone whose journey was not essential to stay at home. Station manager Carl Bossman said

properties had been flooded in the Stokesley, Selby, York and Harrogate areas. "The south of the county continues to be the worst hit."

Flooding also affected Chapel Haddlesey Church of England Primary School, near Selby; and Saxton Church of England Primary School, near Tadcaster.

Parents were asked to listen to local radio bulletins or telephone the schools this morning to ask if they were able to open before sending their children to school.

brian.dooks@ypn.co.uk

Turbulent sea: Visitors brave the wind and rain on Scarborough seafront amid yesterday's storms. Picture: Tony Bartholomew

SIRENS SOUND ALARM AS RESIDENTS TAKE REFUGE

Seventy properties were evacuated in Lincolnshire with a local town hall set up as an emergency centre for residents.

A spokesman for Lincolnshire County Council said flood sirens were being sounded in the area and would continue to sound every 15 minutes for the foreseeable future.

Six schools were closed yesterday and parts of the A1 flooded, with several inches of standing water reported on many roads in Grantham, Lincoln, Louth and Horncastle.

Lincolnshire Fire Service said it had received 600 calls about flooding by mid-afternoon – a figure mirrored in Nottinghamshire.

Residents in several Nottinghamshire villages were battling floods for the second time in four days. In Lowdham, about 300 homes were hit and some residents had to be rescued.

In Mansfield, parts of the A60 were under several feet of water and some businesses were closed. The River Meden broke its banks, closing Hallam,

Thurgarton and North Leverton to traffic.

Nottinghamshire County Council emergency planning manager Sue Storey said: "Our first concern is for the welfare of the people ... who have experienced extensive flash flooding. We are now concerned they are going to be hit by a double whammy as rivers are filled with water from the flash floods.

Action plan for victims of deluge

BRITISH insurers have issued an action plan for home-owners confronted with floods.

Damage from the latest downpour is expected to cost tens of millions of pounds, with the typical flood-related insurance claim reaching £15,000 to £30,000.

In a bid to help those hit by heavy rain, the Association of British Insurers (ABI) offered the following advice:

■ Contact your insurer as soon as possible. Most will offer a 24-hour helpline service to arrange for repairs to be carried out.

■ If necessary arrange for temporary repairs to be made to stop any damage getting worse and keep any receipts.

■ Most insurance policies will cover the cost of alternative accommodation if the damage is so bad that you need to move out for repairs.

■ Do not rush to redecorate as it may take a few weeks for the building to properly dry out.

■ Where there has been flooding, disinfect floors and furnishing. Where practical leave doors, windows and cupboards open.

■ Do not use electricity or water supplies until the all clear is given.

■ Check your motor insurance. Most comprehensive cover will allow driver's to claim against damage to vehicles caused by flooding.

Last week, the Association of British Insurers called on the Government to increase its annual spend on flood defences to £750m.

With adverse weather patterns expected to become more frequent, it also sought a commitment that all schools and hospitals being built are able to cope with the expected environment of 2050.

Jet stream sparks storm

THE wet weather this month is the result of a sluggish jet stream, areas of low pressure and the time of year, forecasters say.

"Waves" in the jet stream which moves weather systems across Britain means areas of low pressure have lasted longer and created far more rain than normal, according to expert Paul Knightley.

The forecaster said that the jet stream usually pulls weather systems along but instead had been holding the low pressure in place.

He said: "Instead of the jet stream blowing straight from the Atlantic across the UK through Scandinavia, it has got huge waves in it.

"In a way it is like a rope which is not nice and straight but has kinks in it, making it move right down to the south and then back up to the north.

"Anything that gets caught by the weather does not have the jet stream to move it along and gets held up in the loop. When the jet stream doesn't push weather systems along, that causes rain and thunderstorms."

Rain is produced when low atmosphere pressure rises and gathers and various weather systems have been moving across the country in recent weeks.

Funnel cloud spotted in Yorkshire

Robert Sutcliffe

OUT for a drive with his mother, civil servant Richard Darn, spotted a dramatic funnel cloud in the distance.

He stopped his car and spent a mesmerising half an hour watching its movement as it gathered together, separated and came back together in a fascinating cycle on Sunday afternoon.

A funnel cloud is a funnel-shaped cloud of condensed water droplets. If one touches the ground it becomes a tornado. Most tornadoes begin as funnel clouds, but many such clouds do not make ground contact and so do not become tornadoes.

Richard, 47, of Barnsley, said: "I was driving around the Penistone area and I said to my mother, (Olive), what she thought it was and she said it looked like a tornado.

"There was another 'storm-chaser' watching with me and taking pictures. He told me it was a funnel cloud and if it touched the ground it would be the first stage in it becoming a tornado."

Go with the flow: A man canoes down a flooded street in Hessle, near Hull, yesterday. Picture: Sean Spencer

Britain battered by rain and gale force winds

NATIONAL
Rob Preece

HUNDREDS of homes were flooded and stricken motorists abandoned their cars as downpours deluged most of England and Wales.

Police closed several roads when a storm band, accompanied by strong to gale force winds, made driving conditions too dangerous.

The Met Office issued severe weather warnings for Wales, the North West, the West Midlands and the South West.

Residents in many of the worst hit areas were still clearing up after floods earlier this month.

Homes in Devon and Gloucestershire were severely affected by the latest onslaught of rain, and the bad weather also disrupted the first day of Wimbledon.

A group of disabled children had a lucky escape after part of a tree crashed through the roof of a minibus in Manchester. Many of the youngsters on

board suffered shock but none was physically injured in the incident.

One motorist had to be taken to hospital after a tree fell on his vehicle on the A277 road, near Exeter.

The 79-year-old man, who was driving a 4x4 vehicle, had to be released by firefighters using hydraulic equipment, but police said

his injuries were not thought to be life-threatening.

Homes in the Devon town of Bideford were hit by flooding up to two feet deep after heavy rain during Sunday night.

In Cheltenham, eyewitnesses reported seeing rivers of flood water flowing through the town centre.

A sports centre in the town

after their bus became stranded in flooding in Lydney, in the Forest of Dean.

RAF Kinloss scrambled a helicopter following reports of a man stuck up a tree in Staveley, Derbyshire.

Police handed out 3,000 space blankets to keep music fans warm as they waited to be picked up by coaches at the Glastonbury Festival.

Tractors had to help pull dozens of cars out of the infamous mud, while others generously helped stranded motorists by pushing their vehicles out of the car parks.

The bad weather also shortened one of the UK's most famous annual academic parades.

The Duke of Edinburgh was scheduled to lead recipients of honorary degrees around Cambridge University's Senate House lawn.

But a downpour forced the dignitaries, who included former United Nations weapons inspector Hans Blix and Bradford-born artist David Hockney, to take a shortcut.

was forced to close after a nearby lake burst its banks.

In nearby Gloucester, firefighters battled to rescue 50 dogs and 20 cats that had become stranded in kennels. The animals were eventually all safely moved to new premises.

Several crashes on the M5 were reported, and about 50 children had to be rescued

Sour note: Music fans wade through the muddy swamp created by torrential rain at the 2007 Glastonbury Festival at Worthy Farm in Pilton, Somerset, yesterday.

Determined: Fans brave the rain on centre court at the Wimbledon tennis championships in London.

Turbulent sea: Visitors brave the wind and rain on Scarborough seafront amid the storms of June 25.

Go with the flow: A man canoed down a flooded street in Hessle, near Hull.

Slow progress:
A car was pushed
through flood
waters by four
men and a
woman in
Barnsley on June
25.

(centre left)
Stranded: A
motorist stuck in
floodwater on
Aldwarke Lane,
Parkgate,
Rotherham,
talked on a
mobile phone
with his head
peering outside
his car. Many
roads in South
Yorkshire had to
be closed.

(centre right) Grim
scene:
Householders
seemed
marooned as they
look out at
flooded streets
following the
heavy rain.

The floods

FOR INFORMATION AND HELP
National Rail inquiries: 08457 484950
Floodline: 0845 988 1188
AA traffic and weather information line: 09003 401 100

Slow progress: A car is pushed through flood waters by four men and a woman in Barnsley yesterday. *Picture: Peter Byrne/PA.*

Emergency after costly clear-up

Second floods in month brings new misery

SOUTH YORKSHIRE

Martin Slack

TORRENTIAL rain brought fresh flood misery to South Yorkshire yesterday as homes and businesses flooded in a deluge for the second time in a fortnight.

In the Dearne Valley, between Barnsley and Doncaster, the River Dearne burst its banks, just days after it overflowed into the centre of the village of Darfield, and roads were closed across the county.

A man who was threatening to jump from a bridge over the M1 at Thorpe Hesley, near Rotherham, added to the morning rush hour chaos as police were forced to close the northbound carriageways.

Later in the day junction 34 of the M1 near Meadowhall was closed completely because of floods, and as traffic slowed to a standstill South Yorkshire Police declared the situation on the roads a "major incident".

Barnsley Council, which last week announced that it had spent hundreds of thousands of pounds clearing up after the previous downpour, said the borough was also in a state of emergency.

The authority, which has set up a hardship fund for those who were not insured for the damage caused last time, provided eight rest centres for residents forced from their homes by the threat of rising floodwaters.

Council leader Steve Houghton described the situation as "unprecedented" and added that because almost every community in the borough had been affected it had been very difficult to deal with.

A Barnsley Council spokesman said: "Our emergency response team received reports of flooding incidents throughout the borough from 8am. A number of roads and bridges were closed and residents were advised to avoid travelling if at all possible."

The rain meant that schools were shut for the day, with 33 closing their doors in Rotherham, 11 in Sheffield and 21 in Doncaster. Two leisure centres were closed by Doncaster Council, which also suspended refuse collections.

Fire crews with an inflatable boat were called out to rescue several motorists, including two men who were stranded in a van at Hague Lane, Wentworth, near Rotherham, and two people who were marooned in Brodsworth, near Doncaster. A fire engine equipped with an aerial ladder platform was also called to an address in Welland Crescent, Elsecar, Barnsley to rescue a couple who had become trapped as floodwater rose up the stairs.

In Sheffield roads throughout the city centre were closed as the River Don burst its banks, and by mid-afternoon Sheffield Council said the transport network was "gridlocked".

A spokesman for the authority said officers had tried to prepare for the worst and added: "On Sunday we put out warning signs for motorists and delivered sandbags to places that were affected by the last floods.

"We are keeping a close eye on the situation and we are closing any roads as and when necessary.

"Extra resources have been put into getting sandbags out and making sure flooded roads are closed."

As the evening rush hour continued, the South Yorkshire Passenger Transport Executive warned commuters of more trouble to come after the bus station at Meadowhall closed.

Sheffield railway station was evacuated for a time and trains from Sheffield to Leeds, Lincoln and Derby were cancelled as were services from Barnsley and Doncaster stations.

Last night the Met Office said that at least three inches of rain would have fallen across South Yorkshire by the end of the day but added that a respite from the worst conditions was expected today.

martin.slack@ypn.co.uk

Stranded: A motorist stuck in floodwater on Aldwarke Lane, Parkgate, Rotherham, talks on a mobile phone with his head peering outside his car yesterday. Many roads in South Yorkshire had to be closed. *Picture: Chris Lawton.*

Grim scene: Householders seem marooned as they look out at flooded streets following the heavy rain in Rotherham. *Picture: Peter Byrne/PA.*

Troubled water: A scene at Barnsley illustrates the appallingly difficult driving conditions for motorists yesterday. The borough council leader described the situation there as 'unprecedented'. *Picture: Peter Byrne/PA.*

Making waves: Vehicles try to negotiate floodwater on Europa Link at Tinsley, Sheffield. The city council said its officers had tried to prepare for the worst in advance on Sunday. *Picture: Chris Lawton.*

Road plight: Drivers stuck in floodwater as the A630 is blocked both ways on Sheffield Road, Conisbrough, Doncaster, after torrential rain brought chaos to the region yesterday. *Picture: Chris Lawton.*

www.yorkshirepost.co.uk

YORKSHIRE POST TUESDAY JUNE 26 2007   5

FOR INFORMATION AND HELP
National Rail Inquiries: 08457 484950
Floodline: 0845 988 1188
AA traffic and weather information line: 09003 401 100

The floods

Elderly and vulnerable left bewildered as deluge puts huge areas underwater

'In bare feet, they paddled in for tea at village hall'

EAST YORKSHIRE

Alexandra Wood

SCORES of elderly and vulnerable residents had to be evacuated yesterday from residential homes across East Yorkshire yesterday as rising floodwaters found their way in.

Homes in Cottingham, Hessle and Market Weighton and sheltered housing in Withernsea were affected, as rain poured relentlessly down from a leaden sky, turning roads into fast-flowing rivers.

In Burton Pidsea, to the east of the city, dozens of homes were evacuated as floodwater inundated half the village.

Villager Marian Willie said: "A lot of the older ones are quite bewildered. There are younger ones too who have lost everything – it's gone right through their houses, 3ft to 4ft of water.

"I've been round to the village hall making tea and they have paddled in in their bare feet. It's so sad to see them."

Last night local authority chiefs were discussing using military vehicles to ferry people from affected areas.

In three hours yesterday morning Humberside Fire and Rescue Service received about 300 calls about flooding. That reached thousands as the day wore on.

By the end of the day massive areas of the region were under water – with some people hit by flooding for the second time in weeks. But this time many more people were directly affected.

Emergency services were sorely stretched as dozens of motorists became trapped in their cars on roads which had turned into deep pools.

People in the Hessle and Willerby areas took their own action to prevent their homes being flooded by erecting a barricade across the end of roads with dustbins to block the wash created by cars.

But as the rain continued – becoming waist-deep in areas of Hessle – others gave up the fight and stood outside their homes in waders and shorts watching the river go by.

Director of customer services at East Riding Council Huw Roberts said the authority had received an average of 2,000 calls per hour. He said: "The priority has been given to those people who are elderly and vulnerable."

People were abandoning cars along main roads like the A1079 Hull to York road – some after realising too late just how deep the water was.

A baby, two other children and a woman had to be carried to safety by firefighters after a car became stuck on Souththorpe Road, in Hull.

Chief Supt Pat Geenty said: "What surprised me was that people just didn't stop – they continued to go into the flood, into the unknown. And then that means we have to find officers who go out and rescue them."

Sqdn Ldr Christopher Mace, who was flying an RAF Leconfield helicopter, said: "The roads are just awash. Where there is a dip then that is where the water is at its deepest."

As the day continued the list of schools, leisure centres, health centres and roads closing lengthened.

The situation got so bad that Humberside Police set up a Silver Command unit at Queens Gardens Police Station to co-ordinate a multi-agency response, including the military.

About half the schools in East Yorkshire ended up closing and by tea-time many of the main roads in Hull were closed.

Police said large areas of the East Riding, including Market Weighton, Bridlington, Goole, Pocklington, Anlaby, Hessle, Withernsea, were affected, as well as Humberston and Cleethorpes in North East Lincolnshire.

A spokeswoman for Humberside Police – moved to Scunthorpe after Priory Road police station was flooded for a second time – said huge areas of East Yorkshire were under water."

Road block: Torrential floodwaters turn the A63 dual carriageway into Hull into a river. Here, vehicles attempt to struggle through near Brough.   Picture: John Jones.

Inundated: Left, the Rose and Crown pub in Beverley, East Yorkshire, surrounded by floodwater while elsewhere residents in the town wade through water left by the deluge.   Pictures: Owen Humphreys/PA.

Grim scene: The makeshift drain cover in which Mr Barnett became trapped is removed.   Pictures: Sean Spencer/PA.

Alert: The scene in Astral Close, Hessle, Hull, as rescuers were desperately trying to save Mr Barnett.

Engulfed by swirling tide of death

Alexandra Wood

NEIGHBOURS last night recounted their desperate attempts to save a 28-year-old trapped in a manhole in Hessle, near Hull, as floodwater engulfed him.

They said they did what they could to help before police divers took over – but it proved impossible as they struggled against the ever rising torrent of water, which by 2pm had reached Mike Barnett's chin.

Sandra Green, one of those who tried to help, said: "The water was rushing around him. I had some breathing apparatus because I am a keen amateur diver.

"When I got there the rising floodwaters were up to the man's chest. We tried to save him but the water was coming up to his shoulders. The police marine rescue team arrived after an hour – they had struggled through the floods and heavy traffic."

Witness Fraser Maude said the man was up to his neck in water when he got to the scene.

"He was clearly distressed and starting to panic. As time went on it was becoming clear he was in difficulty and it was serious. Paramedics were trying to calm him.

"At one point he went under for 20 seconds and they had to drag him back up. You could see his shoulders and head were above the water and then just his face. It was at that point that the emergency services moved us back. We later found out he had died."

Mr Maude said the man was given oxygen while the emergency crews tried to free him.

"Fire crews were going down the street knocking down walls trying to divert the water away from the scene. Other crews were trying to pump water out of the drain," he added.

Chief Supt Pat Geenty, of Humberside Police, said an investigation would be held to determine whether any more could have been done to save the man's life.

But he said: "The fire and rescue service did as much as they possibly could.

"The conditions ... were horrific. The water was rising by the minute."

132

The tidy-up began at the Wicker, Sheffield, after the raging floodwaters left behind a trail of debris and damage. *Picture: Chris Lawton.*

(lower left) Car misery: Vehicles floating by in Sheffield pictured from Sheffield Forgemasters where water is believed to have caused millions of pounds of damage.

(lower right) All change: What a difference a day makes. Drivers had to abandon these two cars where they stood as the swollen River Don burst its banks at the worst of Yorkshire's floods.

(bottom centre) Relieved: Residents who had been trapped in their homes

The floods

FOR INFORMATION AND HELP
National Rail Inquiries: 08457 484950
Floodline: 0845 988 1188
AA traffic and weather information line: 09003 401 100

Flood damage will cost region millions

Yorkshire firms will take months to recover

John Roberts

Mess: The tidy-up begins at the Wicker, Sheffield, after the raging floodwaters left behind a trail of debris and damage.   Picture: Chris Lawton.

THE widespread flooding which devastated Yorkshire will cost the region tens of millions of pounds to recover from according to business and insurance experts.

Business leaders in Yorkshire are warning that firms will take months to get over the damaging effects of the floods as clean up operations began yesterday.

The British Chamber of Commerce said disruption caused to the transport network and people arriving late for work would cost the national economy £400m a day.

Elsewhere, householders affected by flooding are being warned to contact their insurers immediately by an emergency claims specialists based in Yorkshire.

The Harris Claims Group, which has offices in Leeds, is representing clients affected by flooding in both Meadowhall and the Brightside area of Sheffield said spokesman Nigel Parker said the recovery costs for businesses and residents could run into tens of millions of pounds.

Sheffield has been one of the worst affected areas as the heaviest month of rain since records began led to the River Don and Sheaf bursting their banks causing widespread flooding leaving workers trapped on the industrial units in Brightside Lane.

Nigel Tomlinson, the chief executive of the city's Chamber of Commerce said he was worried about firms being unable to meet customer demand while the premises were flooded and he also voiced fears that insurance companies would not be able to cope with the volume of claims.

He said: "Many members businesses have woken up this morning, as we have, to scenes of devastation.

"Clean-ups are under way but this is going to take some time and at some cost.

"Many businesses will not

be operating today and others will be affected for a long time to come. Machinery, stock, buildings and transport infrastructure have all been damaged after becoming submerged in water."

The chamber of commerce was closed yesterday after the ground floor of its office in Saville Street flooded on Monday.

Mr Tomlinson said: "We are trying to help businesses recover from this but we cannot function because we were right in the middle of it. I am worried about a number of businesses in the area who have important order books on the international scene and they won't be able to operate. The impact of this is going to run into tens of millions of pounds."

Insurers are offering advice to householders who have been hit by flooding.

Mr Parker said: "If you are throwing anything away take photographs of it before you get rid of it.

"Once the water has subsided the priority is always to dry out your house as quickly as possible. Get the carpet out of the house and air into it to circulate."

He also warned householders that electrics are likely to have been affected and shouldn't be used immediately after flooding but said comprehensive car insurance would cover any damage to motor vehicles while house insurance policies would cover the cost of alternative accommodation.

Firm facing bill for tens of millions after deluge swept through factory

Paul Whitehouse

Car misery: Vehicles floating by in Sheffield pictured from Sheffield Forgemasters where water is believed to have caused millions of pounds of damage.

ONE of the worst affected companies in Sheffield has estimated the floodwaters which swamped its works caused damage which will cost tens of millions of pounds to rectify.

Sheffield Forgemasters has premises on Brightside Lane which were submerged under six feet of water after the River Don burst its banks, leaving many staff stranded inside a two storey building.

Around 50 workers had no time to escape as water washed through the area and they were left without electricity or telephones.

All had to remain in the building until the early hours of yesterday morning when rescuers arrived using an RAF Sea King helicopter and boats. Twenty were taken to safety, with the remaining 30 staying in the building overnight.

Staff were last night (Tues) starting a clean-up operation at the site as the water level started to recede.

Forgemasters director Peter Birches, who remained on site overnight during the crisis, said: "There are lots of areas on site that are still underwater including cellars and pits containing underground machinery.

"Sludge and oil are covering vast areas throughout the site and we have a huge task ahead of us

All change: What a difference a day makes. Drivers had to abandon these two cars where they stood as the swollen River Don burst its banks at the worst of Yorkshire's floods.

to clean up. There has been major disruption to the site but we are not dead. We will recover. Our primary concern is our employees' health and safety.

"The site is dangerous as there is no lighting, and electricity and water can be a lethal mix. We have sent a number of staff home who

have turned up this morning but key management and maintenance staff are here.

"We are talking damage worth tens of millions of pounds at first glance.

Senior management now plan to raise questions about flood defences in the Lower Don Valley with the authorities responsible.

TRAVEL CHAOS

Roads still closed last night

SOUTH YORKSHIRE
- M1 northbound between J32 M18 and J34 M631
- M1 closed southbound between J36 A61 and J32 M18
- A630 Sheffield Parkway
- A6102 between B6082 and A6109
- A6022 Bridge Street, Swinton
- A6023 Doncaster Road, Denby
- A6125 Sheffield Road, Hoyland
- A60 Sandford Road, Balby
- A630 Sheffield Road, Conisbrough
- A631 Bawtry Road, Tickhill
- A618 Mansfield Road, Aston
- A6109 Meadowhall Road, Sheffield
- A61 Penistone Road, Sheffield

EAST YORKSHIRE
- A63: one lane closed eastbound from A1034 to Ferriby High Road
- A161 Burnham Road, Epworth
- A164, both ways from A15 to B1232

NORTH YORKSHIRE
- A169 Malton Road, Pickering

WEST YORKSHIRE
- B6389 from A638 to A61

Rail lines closed

- GNER services suspended between York and Doncaster, Leeds and Doncaster. A limited road service is in operation but passengers were advised not to travel.
- Hull Trains services suspended between Selby and Doncaster. Trains running Hull to Selby only, then bus to GNER trains at Doncaster.
- Midland Mainline services suspended between Sheffield and Derby, with no road replacement transport.
- Northern routes suspended: Barnley - Huddersfield; Barnsley - Meadowhall; Sheffield - Lincoln; Wakefield Kirkgate - Barnsley; Leeds - Sheffield via Moorthorpe; Doncaster - Hull / Scunthorpe; Leeds - Huddersfield; Sheffield - Doncaster Huddersfield - Wakefield Kirkgate; Knaresborough - York; Hull - Bridlington; Sheffield Grindleford; Leeds - Shipley; Ilkley - Leeds.
- Transpennine Express services suspended between Leeds and Cleethorpes
- Virgin Cross Country services suspended between Derby, Sheffield and Leeds with no road replacement.
- Central trains services suspended between Stockport and Sheffield.

On patrol: Firefighters pass an abandoned car while checking houses in Cliffe Road, Barnsley after the River Dearne broke its banks yesterday.

Relieved: Residents who had been trapped in their homes overnight are rescued in a boat near Rotherham by emergency services.

Dilemma: A river boat breaks loose from her moorings and gets stuck under a gas pipe during the flooding on the River Don in Doncaster.

Homes and businesses wrecked in record downpour

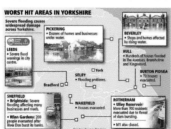

WORST HIT AREAS IN YORKSHIRE

Severe flooding causes widespread damage across Yorkshire.

LEEDS
Severe flood warnings in city centre.

SHEFFIELD
- Brightside: Severe flooding affecting many businesses and roads.
- Winn Gardens: 200 people evacuated after River Don burst its banks.

PICKERING
- Dozens of homes and businesses under water.

BEVERLEY
- Shops and homes affected by rising water.

HULL
- Hundreds of houses flooded in The Avenues, Bransholme and Kingswood.

SELBY
- Flooding problems.

BURTON PIDSEA
- 70 houses evacuated.

WAKEFIELD
- Houses evacuated.

ROTHERHAM
Ulley Reservoir: More than 700 residents evacuated due to threat of dam bursting.
- M1 also closed.

Graphic: Graeme Bandeira

SOUTH YORKSHIRE

Paul Whitehouse

SOUTH Yorkshire will take weeks to recover from the floods which left much of the county, including a large tract of industrial Sheffield and hundreds of homes, under water.

The flooding was a result of the wettest month in the area since records began 125 years ago.

Last night local authorities were only just starting the task of establishing the full extent of the devastation after 24 hours of emergency work, which involved helicopter and boat rescues for those marooned by rising water levels, came to a close.

Even before that started, it was clear that large numbers of businesses and householders had been badly

affected, with local authority officials also expecting widespread damage to the transport system.

One of the most high profile casualties was the Meadowhall shopping centre, which was closed yesterday because of problems with the electricity supply. Staff said it was unclear when it would re-open.

Many roads have been torn up by the force of the water and some bridges and other structures will also require inspections for possible damage before they can be returned to use.

In Sheffield the problems escalated dramatically when the River Don burst its banks, with residents evacuated from the Winn Gardens estate in Middlewood as water spilled towards their homes.

But the effects were much

more widespread in the city centre, where water from the river left the Wicker and many other major traffic routes deep under water all the way to Meadowhall.

Yesterday the shopping centre was closed to the public and many other industrial businesses were also badly affected, reporting repair costs running into many millions of pounds.

Sheffield Council Chief Executive Sir Bob Kerslake described the weather conditions as "unprecedented" but insisted disruption had been kept to the minimum possibly due to good planning and work between the authority and emergency services.

"The conditions of the last day and a half have been exceptional, demonstrating the resilience and courage of all teams involved in dealing

with the problems that have arisen. There has been significant damage to the city of Sheffield, and we now need to take stock. It will take a number of days to assess the extent of the damage, and what actions we need to take.

"Our immediate priority is to get people back in to their homes as quickly and as safely as possible," he said.

Police put out patrols in Winn Gardens to deter looters following incidents in Barnsley where criminals attacked property left unattended because of floods the previous week and similar action took place in Doncaster.

Venues swamped by water include Sheffield Wednesday football club, where the pitch was left submerged and Kelham Island Industrial Museum, where many exhibits were affected.

It will remain closed for the immediate future. In Barnsley, the council describe the floods as "the worst natural disaster in living memory", with up to 600 homes affected and the town's road network left in chaos.

The situation was similar in other parts of the county, with homes evacuated in parts of Rotherham and Doncaster and roads in both towns also badly affected.

Electricity supplies were knocked out to 35,000 homes in Sheffield and some in Rotherham on Monday night and although some supplies were restored after a few hours there were continued problems with power users urged to limit their consumption.

Non-emergency operations at Sheffield Children's Hospital were cancelled as a result.

WEATHER WATCH
Next four days in Yorkshire:
TODAY Heavy showers
THURSDAY Light showers
FRIDAY Sunny intervals
SATURDAY Light rain

www.yorkshirepost.co.uk

YORKSHIRE POST WEDNESDAY JUNE 27 2007 5

FOR INFORMATION AND HELP
National Rail Inquiries: 08457 484950
Floodline: 0845 988 1188
AA traffic and weather information line: 09003 401 100

The floods

M1 shut and villagers flee homes as Victorian reservoir threatens to burst through banks and inundate wide area

Looming threat: Ulley Reservoir after two days of heavy rain, left, and firefighters view the damage where floodwaters have torn away parts of the embankment, above.
Pictures: Owen Humphreys/Simon Hulme.

VILLAGES EVACUATED
ROTHERHAM
Homes cleared — Conkow — A631 — Homes cleared
Junction 33 — Whiston
M1 — To Junction 32
Catcliffe — A618 — Ulley reservoir
Homes cleared
Closed northbound between junctions 32 to 34 and southbound between 36 and 32 — B6067 — Ulley
Aughton — Aston

Crumbling dam still dangerous

Situation 'critical but stable' as Minister sees efforts to halt disaster

Paul Whitehouse

ENGINEERS believed last night they had stabilised a reservoir dam in danger of being breached by millions of gallons of water but the situation remained too dangerous to allow more than 700 evacuated residents to return home.

The residents were alerted in the early hours of yesterday and were taken to a rest centre created at Dinnington Comprehensive School in a fleet of buses.

Checks on Ulley reservoir, a Victorian structure, in Rotherham, revealed flood water had eroded stonework and led to the dam crumbling at one point.

Firefighters had to find pumps with a massive capacity elsewhere in the country and bring them in to reduce the load on the dam and last night the situation was described as "critical but stable" at the reservoir, which covers 36 acres.

In addition to the evacuations, the M1 had to be closed because of the threat from water if the dam burst. An electrical installation supplying power to a large part of South Yorkshire would also be put out of action if the wall failed.

But Rotherham Council spokesman Adam Wilkinson said yesterday the pumping operation was now getting rid of water as fast as it was flowing into the dam.

Thirteen pumps, operated by firefighters from across the country, were being used and more were expected to come into operation later, to start actively reducing the water level.

He said: "The situation is critical and we will know more when we can pump more water out to relieve pressure on the dam.

"We're hopeful it will hold and we're doing everything in our power to make sure it does. There is more rain forecast and that, of course, presents us with further problems. And we are dealing with a 19th century structure."

In addition to pumping out water, engineers had blocked a Victorian spillway with a metal skip, forcing water to exit by a more modern drain where it would not damage the dam.

Among those evacuated was Cyril Hague, 61, of Bank View, Whiston, who said: "There was a helicopter flying overhead a couple of times and that woke me up, then a van came around with a loudspeaker, though I could not make out what it was saying.

"The next thing I knew, a neighbour was banging on my door saying we had to get out. The electrics were off, they had been since 9.30pm the previous day.

"Police came around and told us to get on some buses waiting to evacuate us to Dinnington Comprehensive. I didn't go with the first lot, because I have a neighbour who has had a stroke and I wanted to stay to help her," he said.

At the school a makeshift rescue centre was established in the main hall, using temporary beds and a kitchen set up to provide food and drink.

Washing facilities were also established, with council staff obtaining fresh clothes for those taking shelter there.

"The main problem was that people got bored, although the children were treating it like a big adventure," said Mr Hague.

"There was plenty of food and drink, with the voluntary services, medical people and police all making sure we were well looked after."

Rotherham police commander Chief Superintendent Matt Jukes said the situation downstream was "quite grave".

"But it is a quite stable position. It's not getting worse but it's not getting better. All the important emergency procedures have kicked in."

Asked about the flooding scenario if the dam failed, the officer said: "The engineers are saying there is a possibility of water moving quite quickly."

He said the villages potentially in the path of any dam burst, including Treeton, Catcliffe and Whiston, were already experiencing river flooding yesterday.

Later, Climate Change Minister Ian Pearson arrived at Ulley Dam for himself and stopped to talk to engineers and firefighters.

He said: "There is a serious situation there but I'm confident, the experts are telling me that they are doing all that they can to address it."

Safe: Families take shelter from the dam threat at Dinnington Comprehensive School. Picture: John Giles/PA

Adventure: A youngster makes the best of things in the temporary shelter.

Sea of mud swamped offices and vehicles

Martin Slack

THICK mud covered the pavements, and abandoned cars swept hundreds of yards by floodwater littered the roads in Sheffield's Brightside Lane area.

Council workers in diggers were trying to scoop up the silt and driftwood and others worked to clear the drains, but the devastation left by the swollen River Don was still plain to see.

Cars worth tens of thousands of pounds were full of water and mud while burglar alarms sounded in deserted offices which had been a hive of activity just 24 hours earlier.

At the start of the working day on Monday, no one could have realised the level of damage that would be caused by the rain or imagined the horrendous aftermath.

But yesterday morning, shocked business owners and workers surveyed what was left and wondered how they could ever get back on their feet.

One of the worst-hit premises was the headquarters of national charity Support Dogs, which trains dogs for disabled people at its Bright side Lane base.

Manager Amanda Hutt was forced to evacuate staff and animals from the training centre on Monday afternoon as the river looked set to burst its banks.

When she returned yesterday, the centre, opened just two years ago after a massive fundraising effort, was filled with mud and the force of the flood had demolished the building's back wall.

Mrs Hutt, 32, of Chapel town, Sheffield, said: "I was absolutely devastated when I came down here and saw the state of the building. We have lost everything.

"Two of the staff took the dogs home in a van yesterday and were unable to get back for their cars. Now they are written off. And the building is so badly damaged we can't use it.

"I am just trying to keep it together at the moment for the sake of the staff, but when I get back home I know I'm going to cry for hours."

Businessman Keith Riley was also counting the cost after 6ft of water swept into his engineering workshop alongside the River Don in Meadowhall Road.

Mr Riley, 67, said: "I have lived and worked in Sheffield all my life and I have never seen anything like what we experienced yesterday. I have half a million pounds' worth of equipment in this work shop completely wrecked.

"I don't even know yet if the insurance is going to pay out. The water has knocked down walls all around the building and now I think we will be a target for looters, who have already been looking for ways in."

Gas fitter James Raistrick, 25, was shocked to find his Audi S3 Quattro 300 yards from where it was left on Monday, in the Jessops riverside office development off Brightside Lane.

He said: "The car has got a inch or more of mud all over the leather seats and upholstery and it is definitely a write-off. I don't even know how I am going to get it moved from here. I've only had it three months."

martin.slack@ypn.co.uk

Going: The main road in Catcliffe, Rotherham, where homes and gardens were left under several feet of floodwater. Picture: Chris Lawton.

Going: A caravan floats down the main road in Catcliffe in South Yorkshire.

Gone: The drowned world created by days of torrential rain at Catcliffe, with more bad weather on its way.

(top) Ulley Reservoir on June 26 after two days of heavy rain. *Pictures: Owen Humphreys/Simon Hulme.*

134

Canoes were one way of getting around many places in deluged Yorkshire on June 26. Kenny Inman, whose school was closed for the day, made the most of conditions along with his father Mike in the Market Place in Pickering, North Yorkshire.

(immediately below) Canoeists also took advantage of conditions in the historic East Yorkshire town of Beverley.

6 YORKSHIRE POST WEDNESDAY JUNE 27 2007 www.yorkshirepost.co.uk

The floods

FOR INFORMATION AND HELP
National Rail Inquiries: 08457 484950
Floodline: 0845 988 1188
AA traffic and weather information line: 09003 401 100

Hundreds rescued as water continues to rise

Police warn public not to leave their homes

EAST YORKSHIRE

Alexandra Wood

HUNDREDS of people were rescued yesterday as floodwater continued to rise in parts of Hull and villages to the east of the city.

Police warned that it was "not business as usual" and people should not leave their homes "unless absolutely necessary".

Hundreds more residents were evacuated, rescuers using boats on Hull's Orchard Park estate and in Priory Road and also in Greatcoates and Cromwell Road in Grimsby, where the River Freshney had burst its banks.

In Holderness, water levels were again rising in Burstwick, and officers waist-deep in waders were going from house to house, asking people to leave.

The nearby village of Burton Pidsea would not have looked out of place in Venice, as water inundated 70 homes.

Villagers there have mounted their own clear-up effort, and have even started a fund to help people with no insurance.

Donations for the relief fund at Burton Pidsea can be left at the garage or village hall.

At the village hall, volunteers were handing out tea and sandwiches to evacuees facing a second night away from their homes.

They included Amanda Brooke and Keith Allatt – along with their great dane, mastiff and Staffordshire bull terrier – with a few sparse possessions.

The pair, who rented a house in one of the worst affected parts of the village, are homeless, like many others across the region.

Mr Allatt said: "The people have been fantastic, they have given the dogs food, and blankets, they have fed us and watered us.

"But we have nowhere to go."

Many small lanes in the surrounding areas of East Yorkshire were passable only by 4x4 vehicles.

From the upstairs window of her 19th century converted barn at Elstronwick, now surrounded by a huge lake, resident Angela Fitzpatrick said the flooding was heartbreaking.

She said: "Everybody said they would come as soon as they could – but there's nowhere they can pump the water to."

On Hull's Bransholme estate an unusual rescue operation was being mounted as huge koi carp swam along the streets.

As she loaded large fish into a plastic container in Howdale Road, Jo Waterhouse said: "We are just going to put them in people's ponds – it's better than letting them die."

Resident Linda Lewis walked gingerly on wet carpets and buckling flooring in her house in the aptly named Cormorant Close, in Hull, still trying to make sense of what had happened.

Looking at the tidemarks in her living room, left by the 2ft flood, she said: "It just came that quick.

"Last time the fire brigade came and it went straight away but this time it just flooded up the garden, then suddenly it washed in the house front door and back door."

There were around 200 evacuees yesterday afternoon at Hull City Hall. However, at rest centres in Beverley and Withernsea numbers were less than expected – thanks to the community spirit that has been a feature of the crisis.

"...it just flooded up the garden, then suddenly it washed in the house front door and back door."

Chief Supt Paul Cheeseman warned that the emergency was far from over. He said: "The situation is far worse than people think. The water levels are still rising in some parts of the city.

"It can be tempting for those who do not live in an area that has been affected to think that the water levels are low enough to go about their daily business but we must urge people not to leave their homes unless absolutely necessary."

Lifeboat crews from Redcar and Cleethorpes moved inland yesterday to help rescue people from flooded areas of Hull and Grimsby.

The seven-strong Redcar crew travelled 120 miles to East Yorkshire with a D-class lifeboat and lifesaving equipment to pick up people stranded in west Hull.

Meanwhile RNLI volunteers from Cleethorpes rescued 15 people, including three children, from homes and a community centre on the Willows Estate, Grimsby.

Aftermath of disaster: Canoes were one way of getting around many places in deluged Yorkshire yesterday. Top, Kenny Inman, whose school was closed for the day, makes the most of conditions along with his father Mike in the Market Place in Pickering, North Yorkshire. Above, left and right, canoeists also took advantge of conditions in the historic East Yorkshire town of Beverley.

Alert: Emergency services in Seaton Road, Hessle, near Hull, yesterday where standing water still threatened homes.

Comfort stop: An elderly evacuee enjoys a hot drink as he joins 300 others in temporary respite at Hull City Hall. Picture: Terry Carrott

Devastation: Local residents help clear a cottage in Sinnington village near Pickering after the River Seven burst its banks.

Pumping out: Householders try to clear flood water from their inundated homes in Seaton Road, Hessle, near Hull yesterday.

Still big risk from river in city centre

WEST YORKSHIRE

Joanne Ginley and Fiona Evans

MORE West Yorkshire residents had to be evacuated from their homes as flood waters rose, while others spent the day cleaning up and counting the cost of the damage.

Yesterday river levels fell slightly in the centre of Leeds but last night the Environment Agency warned there was still a serious risk of flooding from the River Aire in the city centre. Officials are hoping further rain keeps away.

Rail services were also disrupted, with trains unable to travel between Leeds and Doncaster. Trains between Leeds and Bradford Forster Square were suspended and people wanting to travel between Leeds and Skipton and Ilkley had to be diverted via Bradford.

Yesterday morning firefighters remained in the Agbrigg area of Wakefield helping residents leave their flooded homes. In some areas water levels reached chest height. Firefighters were still assisting people yesterday morning and helping move people to temporary shelter at Lightwaves Leisure Centre and Wakefield Town Hall.

Especially badly hit were Charles Avenue, Doncaster Road, Frederick Street and Warwick Street.

Yesterday police warned motorists to take note of diversion signs in Doncaster Road at Ackworth and urged them to find an alternative route.

Eleven schools were shut in Wakefield and eight in Leeds yesterday. Some road closures were also in place yesterday, including Lock Lane, Castleford and the A638 Doncaster Road, from Agbrigg Road to Black Road. A diversion was in place on the A638 at Ackworth.

At 7.50am yesterday firefighters rescued three adults and a cat trapped inside a home in Barnsdale Road, Allerton Bywater, by flood waters.

Monday's floods hit many pockets of West Yorkshire including Mirfield, Liversedge, Cleckheaton, South Elmsall, Brighouse, Pontefract, Castleford, part of Leeds and Wakefield. In some places waters had receded or were pumped out and people were able to go back and survey the extent of the damage.

Up to 130 properties are believed to have been flooded in Leeds with the worst-hit areas being the Dunhills Estate in east Leeds, where 70 properties were flooded by Wyke Beck. It is the third time in as many years that homes have flooded in the area.

About 30 homes were flooded at Millbeck Green in Collingham and about 30 at Kippax. Parts of central Leeds flooded around the Brewery Wharf area and at Lower Wortley.

Residents are being offered support and advice on environmental health, insurance, social services and housing. Leeds City Council has also set up a cleaning service for affected properties and is providing skips.

Fearnville Leisure Centre, in Oakwood, will remain open for people evacuated from their homes in the city.

Half of town marooned after beck bursts its banks

Wading in: Fire crews brought in from Scarborough check stranded vehicles and flooded properties in Pickering, which was under water. Pickering Beck burst its banks, flooding shops and businesses. Picture: Tony Bartholomew.

NORTH YORKSHIRE

Mark Branagan

THE market town of Pickering awoke to find homes, shops and businesses swamped yesterday after what North Yorkshire firefighters said was "possibly the busiest 24 hours in living memory".

Emergency workers pleaded with motorists to steer clear of the flooded town centre after many drivers ignored warnings about the normally busy A169 and A170 being closed through the town.

Pickering town centre was deluged as the beck burst its banks. Homes were evacuated and residents taken to Lady Lumley's School for safety. In the nearby village of Sinnington the River Seven also overflowed, flooding properties and farmland.

Stephen Knight and his family found themselves homeless only four months after moving into their new £275,000 house, a former railway property on The Ropery.

Mr Knight, 55, who manages a building contract business, says he never dreamed the house would be at risk when he moved in with his son Matthew, 23, daughter Helen, 21, and Helen's boyfriend Mark Winspear.

He said: "We have only just got the house as we wanted and decorated the downstairs. There is a flood barrier around the house but the water got over it and started seeping through the walls about 10pm on Monday. In no time at all there was six inches of water all over the house.

"I could not get hold of my son so I rang him to tell him his Xbox was floating out the door thinking that would get him home. Actually we had taken it upstairs.

"Then we went to bed. There was nothing else we could do apart from look out the window at the coastguards, who we do not often see in Pickering, and the firemen. We got a call shortly after 7am asking if we had been flooded and found the water was up to the second tread of the stairs.

"Half of Pickering was marooned. We shut our company because people could not get in. The school is closed and half the market place – about six or eight shops – are under water. The worst affected is the Chinese restaurant, The Fortune Inn.

"But there is an amazing amount of people wandering around the town and morale is good."

North Yorkshire fire service said yesterday the volume of calls had gone down as the weather had improved but they were still on red alert because of the height of rivers and other waterways.

'This has possibly been the busiest period for the North Yorkshire Fire Service in living memory.'

They were still helping householders flooded out in Pickering and there were also problems in the Selby area, where four fire engines were helping at a number of premises with flooding.

Fire control room staff received over 1,000 calls during Monday's heavy rainfall, with requests for help coming in by the minute from hotspots such as Ryedale, Selby, York and Harrogate.

Fire service station manager Carl Boasman said: "This has possibly been the busiest period for the North Yorkshire Fire Service in living memory. Control room staff have worked continuously for the last 24 hours.

"We have had over 30 fire appliances, 150 firefighters, six specialist appliances and over 20 officers and support staff working tirelessly to provide an effective emergency response."

During Monday night firefighters responded to over 200 calls and dealt with flooding in over 400 premises.

In Pickering the Community Junior, Lady Lumley's and St Joseph's RC Primary Schools were closed, as were Sinnington, Thornton Dale C of E and Boroughbridge Primaries. Stokesley School was open only to pupils taking exams.

www.yorkshirepost.co.uk

The floods

FOR INFORMATION AND HELP
National Rail Inquiries: 08457 484950
Floodline: 0845 988 1188
AA traffic and weather information line: 09003 401 100

The devastation from the air

Deserted homes: Uninhabitable houses in the village of Thorpe Audlin.

Hazardous waste: Flood waters swept through this sewage works near Rotherham.

Rain stopped play: Submerged pitch at Sheffield Wednesday's Hillsborough stadium.

Marooned: Meadowhall shopping centre was cut off from the rest of the city

Householders' heartbreak: Homes at Catcliffe lie under six feet of filthy water.

Scene of devastation: The sheer scale of the flooding left homes, businesses, roads, railways and farmland near Rotherham under water.

Road to nowhere: The deserted M1 near Rotherham empty of traffic and surrounded by flooded fields.

Pictures: Glen Minikin/Owen Humphreys

Scene of devastation on June 26: The sheer scale of the flooding left homes, businesses, roads, railways and farmland near Rotherham under water.

(top left) Deserted homes: Uninhabitable houses in the village of Thorpe Audlin.

(second down from top) Hazardous waste: Flood waters swept through the sewage works near Rotherham.

(third down) Rain stopped play: Submerged pitch at Sheffield Wednesday's Hillsborough stadium.

(fourth down) Marooned: Meadowhall Shopping Centre was cut off from the rest of the city.

(fifth down) Householders' heartbreak: Homes at Catcliffe lay under six feet of filthy water.

(bottom) Road to nowhere: The deserted M1 near Rotherham empty of traffic and surrounded by flooded fields.

8 YORKSHIRE POST WEDNESDAY JUNE 27 2007 www.yorkshirepost.co.uk

The floods

FOR INFORMATION AND HELP
National Rail Inquiries: 08457 484950
Floodline: 0845 988 1188
AA traffic and weather information line: 09003 401 100

They never let me anywhere near trapped boy, says anguished father

Residents accuse crews of botching rescue

Alexandra Wood

THE father of a man who died after his foot got stuck in an open drain told yesterday how he would have asked medics to amputate his son's limb if it meant they could free him.

Michael Barnett, a retired panel beater, rushed to Astral Close in Hessle, near Hull, after learning that his son, also called Michael, had become stuck in neck-high water.

He was turned away by police, and returned home, switched on his television and immediately learned of his son's death.

He said. "The television said 'Young man trapped in drain has died' I just turned the telly off.

"I didn't want to believe it, but I suppose I knew I had lost him."

He added. "I would have done anything to save him. I wasn't allowed to go anywhere near and now I will never see him again."

Angry residents yesterday accused emergency services of botching the rescue effort.

Neighbours say heavy lifting gear should have been brought in earlier to extricate Mr Barnett, who died after being stuck in a grate for hours in the neck-high water.

Andrew Claxton, who was with Mr Barnett for two hours until police told him to leave the scene, said the 28-year-old might have lost a leg – but "there was a good chance that they would have got him out alive"

Mr Claxton, who owns nearby fish business Kingston Koi Company, where Mr Barnett worked for 12 years, said. "There were too many chiefs and not enough Indians.

"As neighbours we have lived with the dyke for 40 years. We knew exactly what needed doing but they wouldn't listen. We had the same problem 10 days ago and we got a digger in and pulled the grate out.

"What's upsetting me was the fact he was there for three hours still alive and they brought a digger after four and a half hours to recover the body."

Mr Claxton said Mr Barnett, of Willerby Road, Hull, who was trying to clear a blocked drain during Monday's flooding, was a "hard-working, conscientious lad who would do anything for anyone.

"He did it to save other people – he thought it was the right thing to do."

Chief Supt Pat Geenty said emergency services "tried desperately hard" but the torrent of water coming down the drain made rescue extremely difficult. A file would be prepared for the coroner.

He said: "Everyone is asking how something like this can happen.

"We are going to investigate it fully. We are going to look at the whole circumstances – how the young man got there and what we did."

Glenn Ramsden, of Humberside Fire and Rescue, said they would await the outcome of the investigation. He said: "We thought we carried out a very concentrated rescue effort and unfortunately nature beat us on this occasion."

Horror: The drain in which Michael Barnett, 28, from Hull, died when he became stuck in neck-high water on Monday. Picture: Sean Spencer.

Tributes: Flowers left in Astral Close, Hessle, in memory of tragic Michael Barnett, right. Picture: Terry Carrott

Pensioner died after waters rose under rail bridge

Martin Slack

POLICE last night revealed more details about the death of a 68-year-old man, who was overwhelmed by floodwaters in Sheffield.

Officers believe the man, who has not yet been named, was returning to his home in the Burngreave area when he was caught out by rising water levels at about 8pm on Monday.

Detective Chief Inspector Steve Williams, who is leading the inquiry for South Yorkshire Police, said the incident had been a "tragic" loss of life and appealed for witnesses who may be able to help piece together what happened.

Police believe they have identified the man, but said they could not disclose his name until his relatives had been informed. They are not treating the death as suspicious.

It is thought he was walking along Carlisle Street, past its junction with Newhall Road, in the Brightside area of Sheffield, when he came to a natural dip beneath a railway bridge.

Mr Williams said. "The water rose extremely quickly. The victim was with another man and the water level rose from ankle deep to chest deep. Soon both men were swimming and trying to pull themselves along the side of the bridge wall.

"However, the 68-year-old got into difficulties. The other man tried to assist him but was unable to pull the victim from the flood. But he did get to the side and was able to call for help."

It is believed that several passers-by then became involved, with one man spending several minutes underwater, eventually locating the unconscious pensioner and dragging him to dry land.

Paramedics took him to Sheffield's Northern General Hospital, but he was pronounced dead on arrival.

Officers would like people involved in the rescue attempt, or those who may have seen what happened before the water level rose, to come forward.

Anyone with information should contact Detective Sergeant Graham Stead on 0114 296 4171.

River tragedy schoolboy was 'so loveable'

Flood victim: Ryan Parry, 14, who died when he fell into the River Sheaf at Millhouses in Sheffield.

Paul Whitehouse

THE parents of a teenager who drowned after being swept away by the River Sheaf in a Sheffield park have spoken of their loss.

Mandy and Chris Parry described their son Ryan, 14, whose body was found hours after he disappeared from Millhouses Park as "so loveable he was unbelievable"

He had apparently been taking a short cut home with friends from King Ecgbert School after buses stopped running because of Monday's floods.

In a statement they said he "was a kind boy who always put everyone before himself"

"Ryan enjoyed everything and was very popular with both older and younger children. Children came knocking on the door wanting to play with him."

The river is believed to have been flowing at speeds in excess of 20mph when the tragedy happened.

A 16-year-old friend said: "The school buses had been taken off because of the weather and the main road was flooded.

"Nothing like this has ever happened before so he must have been walking through the park to get home. He normally catches a school bus which drops him off near his home.

"People were being stopped walking along the main road which was flooded and were told to go through the park.

"He went into the park and had no idea it was flooded as well. The river had overflowed onto the paths.

"He was with some friends but nobody knew how fast the water was flowing. Ryan just got pulled into the river by the current.

"His friends tried to get him out but the water was flowing too fast for them and they could not reach him."

Ryan's body was later found a quarter of a mile downstream.

'Nobody knew just how fast the water was flowing. Ryan just got pulled in the river by the current.'

His friend said: "He was probably walking through the park to see if there were any buses further up the hill running to his home. He and his friends thought it was the safest place to go.

"You wouldn't think the park could flood, it is normally full of people.

"He is not the sort who liked to mess about and was a quiet and sensible lad who kept himself to himself.

"It's a real tragedy. Ryan is only small and wouldn't have stood a chance in the water."

Bob Evans, headteacher of King Ecgbert School said: "It was with sadness and shock that we heard about the tragedy involving Ryan. Our condolences and sympathy go to Ryan's family at this very difficult time.

"Ryan was a lively and popular pupil with many friends.

"The school community is shocked."

Special assemblies were held at the school to inform pupils of the incident and counselling sessions were being held.

South Yorkshire Police investigating the circumstances surrounding Ryan's death have made an appeal for anyone with information to contact DC Jo Smithson on 0114 2963660.

Deluged home-owners submit 8,000 insurance claims in 24 hours – and firms brace themselves for more to come

Maggie Stratton

MORE than 8,000 insurance claims were made in 24 hours by home-owners across Britain hit by torrential downpours.

And since around 120 flood warnings were still in place across the country late yesterday – 25 of them classified as severe – insurers were bracing themselves for further claims.

In Worksop, Nottinghamshire, the town centre was sealed off and 70 properties were evacuated as flood waters rose.

In Lincolnshire, the Environment Agency opened embankment gates along the River Witham at Saxilby and Bassingham to redirect water onto nearby fields. Residents in a nearby 20-storey block of flats were evacuated as a precaution.

"If the gates were not there, Lincoln would have been flooded by now," an agency spokeswoman said.

Elsewhere in Lincolnshire, more homes were evacuated in Louth and Wainfleet.

In Derbyshire, people were moved out of around 60 properties in Chesterfield as the rivers Rother and Hipper burst their banks.

Dozens of people were evacuated from their homes in Ludlow, in Shropshire, when a bridge collapsed, severing a gas main and causing minor explosions.

The River Corve washed away a 40ft section of a main road leading into Ludlow.

In nearby Tenbury Wells, 20 people were forced to leave their homes when the River Teme burst its banks.

The Cotswold town of Stroud was deluged, some streets under more than two feet of water. Cars were seen bobbing in the flooded streets as water ran off nearby hills into the town.

Properties in Gloucester, Tewkesbury and Cheltenham were also hit.

Fire crews in Gloucestershire rescued a total of 88 people, including children trapped on a school bus.

Tony Blair praised the efforts of the emergency services and offered sympathy to those who lost loved ones in the floods.

Speaking at a Downing Street news conference, he said: "Our flood defences are holding but this is a difficult situation and it is not the first time over the past few years that we have been subject to quite unusual and extraordinary weather variations."

BOY KILLED BY FALLING TREE

A primary school head spoke of his "devastation" after a 10-year-old boy was killed on an activity holiday yesterday.

Three other pupils were injured when a tree branch fell as they took part in an orienteering exercise at Felbrigg, Norfolk.

The youngsters were among a group of more than 50 pupils from Heathlands Primary School in West Bergholt, Essex.

Police were trying to establish whether high winds were a factor in the tragedy.

Headteacher John Watts described the youngster who died as a "fantastic little boy"

Wading through: A resident tries to make his way down Market Street in Tenbury Wells in Worcestershire, flooded by the River Teme. Picture: David Davies/PA Wire

Farmers fear for crops and livestock

Maggie Stratton

WITH huge swathes of farmland submerged across Yorkshire, the National Farmers Union was yesterday inundated with calls about damaged and ruined crops and stranded livestock.

Wheat, pea and potato crops were among the worst hit by the torrential rains and flooding, the NFU said.

And even where land was not flooded, there were fears that vast amounts of crops have been ruined by the heavy rainfall.

"We have had reports of entire farms being completely underwater. We've had a call from one farmer in Atwick on the coast where 90 acres of wheat has been lost," an NFU spokeswoman said.

Wheat fields are collapsing across the region as the crops soak up massive amounts of water in the wake of Monday's deluge.

Once crops collapse they become difficult to harvest and further problems can be caused by flattened crops resprouting.

"At the moment, I think we are really talking about a drop in quality, particularly for milling wheat which may mean it is no longer suitable for milling, but only for feed. What people are saying is that if it dries up, then we are not necessarily going to get crops lost," the NFU spokeswoman added.

East Yorkshire is home to large numbers of pea crops and, with the harvest just beginning, there is concern that land will be too waterlogged for harvesting machinery to operate.

Continuing wet conditions are also a danger to potato crops, increasing the risk of potato blight.

The Royal Agricultural Benevolent Institution (RABI) said it was preparing to provide support to those farmers badly affected.

Chief executive Paul Burrows said: "The torrential rain has caused considerable hardship in many rural areas as well as towns and cities. Many farming families may be in need of immediate support."

The RABI welfare department can be contacted on 01865 727888.

Horror: The drain in which Michael Barnett, 28, from Hull, died when he became stuck in neck-high water on Monday, June 25.

(continued in text)

www.yorkshirepost.co.uk   YORKSHIRE POST WEDNESDAY JUNE 27 2007   13

Focus

Going, going...
Tom Richmond on Tony
Blair's long goodbye **15**

Today's TV
Your complete
programme guide **16**

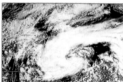
Under a cloud: A satellite picture of the UK at noon on Monday.

Why did this day of summer deluge take us by surprise?

Was the rain
which left much
of Yorkshire
underwater just a
freak of nature or a
sign of worse
things to come?
Chris Benfield
reports.

IT was towards the end of last week that the Meteorological Office started sending out messages saying that unusual weather was on the way. It was Friday when the message hardened into: watch out for Monday.

It was not as precise a forecast as you would have liked if you were working on flood prediction for the Environment Agency or on mop-up preparations for the fire and rescue services, the local authorities, the rail companies, the highways authorities and the other agencies which started staffing up for an emergency watch on Sunday night.

"The Met Office is good at saying what will happen but exactly where and exactly when it still up to the gods," summed up one of its clients yesterday.

The Friday warning was based on an "ensemble forecast" – the pooling of information from several agencies in several countries, which burned into a map of the things which make our weather: air pressure, air temperature, air direction and water vapour.

It's a three-dimensional map and at the top of it is the jet stream, the complex of winds which whistles constantly around the outer edges of the atmosphere, five miles above our heads, driven by the rotation of the planet and the power of the Sun and interfered with by lower-level exchanges between cold from the poles and heat from the tropics, all stirred around by the oceans.

The winds down here conflict with the winds up there and depending on the height of the column of air above us, and its temperature, we are almost always in an area of higher pressure or lower pressure than the average.

Nature tries to even things out, but never quite goes there. And so, on the old-fashioned weather maps we used to see on television, and which the meteorologists still pore over behind the scenes, there are always "fronts", where one set of conditions hits another – and the

trouble starts. The jet stream tends to keep things moving from west to east. But for a thousand reasons, it has been sluggish this month in our latitudes. Fronts have come to us and stayed, locked in position or moving very slowly, while people and crops have been dying from heat and drought in Italy and Greece, Romania and Bulgaria.

The brilliant nine days at the start of June in England, now forgotten, powered a lot of water into the atmosphere as vapour and it was still all waiting to come down again when it hit the cold up above. The result was the two weeks of steady rain, and occasional torrents, which soaked the ground and prepared the way for Wet Monday.

Meanwhile, another low-pressure lump of sodden air was moving in from the east-north-east – the worst possible direction for Yorkshire. If it had come the other way, as usual, the Pennines would have interfered. As it was, we had an exceptional summer storm only four days after the one before.

"It was the hardest kind of event to read," says Robin Bailey, the Environment Agency strategist who co-ordinated the North East flood warning operation from a room full of computers in Park Square, Leeds.

"In winter, you get a fairly predictable build-up over 24-48 hours. The snow-melt and the rain comes down from the hills and you

can see the river rising in Skipton before it gets to Leeds, for example.

"This time, there was nothing exceptional happening up there. Leeds was flooded with water falling on Leeds. Howardens, a city like Leeds is 90 per cent impermeable. The rain runs straight into the watercourses and the drains and the effect is instant."

The Hull Valley, just inside the coastal boundary which played its part in the equations, took 100mm of rainfall. Its annual average is 600mm. So that was one-sixth of it in a day – half an inch an hour for 12 hours. At the end of the day, the rainfall for the June days so far this

year had risen to 161 per cent of the average for the month, according to climate-uk.com, a website run by Philip Eden, BBC consultant and author of several books on British weather.

That, everyone agrees, is exceptional – and possibly record-breaking. But the reliable records do not go back very far. There have been comparable days. There have been comparable months. There have almost certainly been comparable Junes. Other parts of the world deal with worse every year. Professional weather watchers are wary of fitting one event into the argument for global warming.

Philip Eden said in a comment in this newspaper on the 2005 floods: "Every time the weather turns nasty, we seem to think it is something new. But it's not.

"Most of us now live in centrally-heated homes, work in environmentally-controlled offices or factories, and drive around in comfortable motor cars which protect us from the wind and rain.

"We are becoming divorced from our environment. We don't notice the weather unless it actually penetrates our cocoon and disrupts our daily routine. When that happens, we get annoyed.

"A weather event which may happen half a dozen times in any given year is a freak of nature

which demands some sort of explanation."

Nowadays, however, it takes a maverick to say global warming has nothing to do with anything. Step forward, in that role, Piers Corbyn, managing director of Weather Action (weatheraction.com), a service based on the theory that weather on Earth is driven entirely by the rhythms of the Sun.

Corbyn makes a living out of applying the theory to long-range forecasting and has been right enough then to make it hard to dismiss him.

He claimed yesterday that his customers were warned weeks ago of a downpour between June 24 and 26, because of solar activity. And he was already predicting something similar – "severe thunderstorms, hail and floods" – over July 4-5 and July 10-11. The second episode would be the worst, but the centre of it would probably be further south than this one, as far as England was concerned, he said.

"I've been trying to get through to the right people in Rotherham to tell them they had better have that dam fixed by then." he added.

"This is the start of a pattern of exceptional weather events which we see every 30 to 34 years."

Back at the Met Office, the experts in more conventional forecasting are more reluctant to commit themselves further ahead than this weekend. A Manchester-based

spokesman, Alan Goodman, said: "Wednesday and Thursday should give us nothing worse than showers, although some will be heavy, but there is yet another unsettled pattern moving in for the weekend. We can hope it will not mean anything as severe or persistent as we have just seen, but the possibility is there."

Nothing can be done before then to stop the water. Nothing is likely to be done before it happens all over again next year. Long-term, all the computerised readings at the Environment Agency will probably lead to some more engineering work – and some major investment in the Victorian drainage systems run by the water companies and the local authorities is long overdue – but short-term, the emphasis is on giving people enough warning to move their valuables.

Down by the River Aire in Leeds on Monday evening, after three Severe Flood Warnings had been voicemailed out, residents of the upmarket village which has sprung up along the riverside were not using their mobile phones to film the river lapping at their courtyards, where their nice new cars were still parked.

Robin Bailey observes: "Damned if we do and damned if we don't," he observes. "We can't stop the weather. We can only try to warn everyone what it is going to do."
chris.benfield@ypn.co.uk

> "We don't notice the weather unless it actually penetrates our cocoon and disrupts our daily routine. When that happens, we get annoyed."

Water wheels: A cyclist wades through Monday's flood waters in Leeds city centre.   Picture: Simon Hulme

---

Never mind the floods, Yorkshire's resilience is home and dry

Monday's
downpour failed to
dampen traditional
Yorkshire grit, says
Stephen Biscoe

THE unprecedented downpour on Monday which transformed becks, streams and stream into raging torrents, threatened the dam retaining the 35-acre Ulley reservoir and claimed at least three lives has turned Yorkshire into a disaster area.

Each part of it – north, south, east and west – is having to cope with the consequences as hundreds of householders face heartbreaking discoveries of how much damage they have suffered.

Businesses, too, are having to assess their losses, and in some cases these may be so great that recovery is impossible.

But at least the region has the comfort of knowing that the concern is. He told a Downing Street news conference that the floods across northern England had been an "extraordinary and very serious event" And although some might think it warranted a ministerial visit, at least there is the satisfaction of knowing that the Environment Secretary David Milliband made a statement in the Commons about it.

Some MPs – those who hadn't dropped off to sleep or were engaged elsewhere at the time – will, therefore, be fully appraised of what the region has been

through, and the difficulties that lie ahead.

That the region will need financial assistance from the Treasury is a foregone conclusion, meaning, of course, that the Treasury will um and ah and look for any excuse not to give any.

There is, then, good reason to be grateful for something called "Yorkshire grit".

Some might say it is evidence at the height of the calamity when the stoic, phlegmatic spirit which defines the Yorkshire character came to the fore.

The scenes of devastation in

Sheffield were described by police and city council representatives at a news conference yesterday as "unprecedented" – the Environment Agency described them as "off the scale" – and at the same time, tribute was paid to the resilience of the emergency services and the people of Sheffield.

A man woken at 3am by police because his house was in danger if the Ulley dam should break epitomised that spirit when he spoke to a radio reporter from the refuge he and his family had been directed to at Dinnington Comprehensive School: yes, it

had been rather alarming to be woken at such an hour; no, he and his family had not been able to rescue anything when they left their home, having only enough time to throw on some clothes, and no, he was not especially anxious.

His tone was that of someone who had been through an unusual experience, but not an especially upsetting one. Yet, in truth, he and his family faced calamity.

Residents in the Avenues area of west Hull demonstrated a self-help approach by blocking their flooded streets to prevent vehicles using them and creating a wash which would have swept water over front door steps and into their homes.

Getting no assistance from the council by way of sandbags or the like, they hit and not been able to closing the affected roads, one group collected up some barriers which had been left in a street near by and used them to stop the traffic.

Others used their cars for the same purpose, and when the police objected, invited them to tow the cars away.

Commonsense prevailed, and the cars were allowed to remain.

In the Wicker area of Sheffield near the River Don, where the flood

water left a record of its height on the walls of buildings, traders were said in one report to be putting on a brave face as they cleared water and sludge from their premises.

At such times, there is a certain camaraderie in the face of adversity which helps individuals cope; but never let it be thought that the smiles which are sometimes seen in newspaper and television pictures of people caught up in a flood in any way reflect the true effect of what has befallen them.

Behind the brave face is often inexpressible dismay, and often trauma is waiting its cue in the wings.

Floods such as those which Yorkshire experienced on Monday deliver immediate disruption, immediate destruction and immediate tragedies, and in the aftermath, long-term ruination of homes, businesses and lives. With the likelihood of increasingly extreme weather conditions bringing more frequent and more violent floods, the Government must divert the resources needed to help stricken areas and to build sufficient flood defence systems to provide new levels of protection.

These are not some kind of luxury which can be pushed down

the list of priorities for Government spending; they are essential now, and the need for them will become greater with every passing year.

The Government must also show clear leadership in terms of where developers are allowed to put new housing estates, and what precautions must be taken to reduce the risk of flooding.

The demand for new homes is such that developers and local planning authorities will increasingly turn their attention to low-lying areas which have not previously been built on for the very good reason that they are low lying.

To ignore the risk this poses would be sheer madness.

The events on Monday across Yorkshire are an intimation of what lies in store over the coming decades. A stoic determination to get on with life when water's lapping the doorstep, or two inches of filthy mud are spread across office floor, or the railway station is flooded and not a single train is running, is admirable. It will not, however, make the long-term difference which is now becoming absolutely vital.

stephen.biscoe@ypn.co.uk

Carrying on regardless: Two workers in Leeds.

Water wheels:
A cyclist waded
through flood
waters in Leeds
city centre.

This frightened dog was rescued in the village of Toll Bar, near Doncaster, where floodwater rose alarmingly high. Firefighters using dinghies got to the house of a woman who owned two dogs. Clutching one of them, she was helped into the boat and taken to safety. Her other dog was taken on board a second boat before the owner and her pets were reunited on dry land. *Picture: Lewis Whyld/PA.*

Safe: A resident is helped from her home at Kingswood in Hull. *Picture: Terry Carrott.*

---

www.yorkshirepost.co.uk

YORKSHIRE POST THURSDAY JUNE 28 2007   3

The floods

Pet rescue...
It was bad enough for the people, but spare a thought for their terrified pets. This frightened dog was rescued in the village of Toll Bar, near Doncaster, where floodwater rose alarmingly high. Firefighters using dinghies got to the house of a woman who owned two dogs. Clutching one of them, she was helped into the boat and taken to safety. Her other dog was taken on board a second boat before the owner and her pets were reunited on dry land.
Picture: Lewis Whyld/PA.

Further storms to batter Britain

Tom Smithard and Emily Seymour

THE worst-hit parts of Yorkshire need to brace themselves for another battering from torrential rain, the Met Office said yesterday.

Forecasters are now predicting up to 78mm of rain will fall tomorrow and at the weekend across the region. They issued an early warning of severe weather and said the rain would result in further disruption –especially to communities already hit hard by this week's downpours.

Friday will bring 25mm of rain across Wales, the Midlands and the North. But the main concern comes from another weather system likely to bring 50mm of rain over on Saturday or Sunday.

The rain is expected to start on Saturday afternoon and continue to get heavier throughout Sunday. Temperatures will be cold for June – between 13C and 16C, but possibly rising just a couple of degrees.

"This further rainfall, on top of what has already been a record breaking wet June for some will only add to the problems being faced across parts of England and Wales.

"The hardest hit areas are likely to see further significant rainfall only exacerbating the existing flooding," said a spokesman.

Rain falls badly on the flood plains, say critics

Agency experts warned against building homes in at-risk zones

Simon Bristow

THE landscape may not be permanently scarred when the waters recede but there are some who will be hoping it is at least sufficiently changed to cover their tracks.

Critics of urban planning say it should come as no surprise that two of the residential areas in the region worst affected by Monday's heavy rain – Catcliffe, near Rotherham, and Kingswood in Hull – were built on flood plains.

Both sites have again proved extremely vulnerable, causing misery to residents and prompting frantic and costly attempts to evacuate them from their homes.

Kingswood resident Ivor Mills, who has been staying with relatives, said: "We've been under water for the last three days – my house is totally gutted. My laminate flooring is floating and my cupboards are swimming: it's just ruined."

Less than two years ago this newspaper revealed that millions of homeowners were facing an increased risk of flooding because properties were still being built on flood plains despite warnings from experts.

The Environment Agency, a statutory consultee to planning authorities, was so concerned that it introduced new guidelines last December specifically warning against building on flood plains. Of the 3,690 planning applications it was consulted over in Yorkshire and the North East in 2005-6, about 1,800 concerned areas at risk from flooding.

Safe: A resident is helped from her home at Kingswood in Hull.   Picture: Terry Carrott.

The agency objected to 330 projects in Yorkshire in that time and councils followed its advice in all but 23 cases.

A spokesman said most of these concerned minor projects, such as home extensions and barn conversions. About five or six were new build and only one – for 14 houses near Goole – was on any significant scale. This was thought to be still going through the planning process.

Tony Mannion, an Independent Tory councillor in Rotherham, said entire communities were paying the price for the follies of the past. He said: "You should not build on flood plains. Flood plains are there for a reason – to cater for a rapid expansion of water.

"We have had flooding before in Catcliffe and if the weather patterns are changing we need to look again at where we build and our flood defences."

Phil Rothwell, head of flood policy at the Environment Agency, said Government spending to protect homes on flood plains should be increased from £600m a year to £750m, with that figure rising to £1bn in the future.

Others say development should take place elsewhere.

John Fareham, chairman of Hull Council's planning committee, said: "It's pretty self-evident. If you build on flood plains this is what happens. It's a national problem and what we've got to look at is our land use in this country. Developers and builders are going to have to get used to redeveloping brownfield sites."

Jeremy Walker, chairman of the Yorkshire Flood Defence Committee, said: "Here we have had another wake-up call that we have got to do more to adapt to the changing climate, and that includes adapting more through the planning system as well as providing more investment in flood defences to property and infrastructure."

Businesses count cost and appeal to Goverment

Lizzie Murphy

FLOODING could cost Sheffield's biggest brewery more than £100,000 to put right after the River Don burst its banks.

Kelham Island Brewery, which is close to the river near Sheffield city centre, is one of the thousands of companies counting the cost of this week's unprecedented rainfall, which will run into millions of pounds worth of damage and lost trade.

But help has been offered in the form of a £500,000 interest-free emergency fund, which is being set up by the South Yorkshire branch of the Federation of Small Businesses.

Chairman Tony Cherry said: "Big businesses tend to have the infrastructure and contacts to obtain the assistance they require in these circumstances while small enterprises are left to fund for themselves or seek help from organisations such as the FSB which will make every effort to provide assistance wherever possible."

Companies across Sheffield, Doncaster, Rotherham, East Yorkshire and Pickering in North York shire have been hit by floods.

Sheffield's Master Cutler Alan Reid yesterday appealed to Gordon Brown to introduce 100 per cent capital allowances to help companies. Sheffield Chamber of Commerce, which was engulfed by water, is also calling for Government aid to help businesses.

Dave Wickett, owner of Kelham Island brewery and the Fat Cat pub, said he was losing £10,000 worth of business a week and would be £25,000 a week worse off in total.

He said he had lost 50,000 pints of beer from his flooded cellar, adding: "The worst thing is not knowing how if is going to affect the brewery in the long term. I hope our customers don't find other suppliers while we are out of production.

Meadowhall remained closed and without power and will remain closed again today. A spokeswoman said it would reopen in stages.

The floods

FOR INFORMATION AND HELP
National Rail Inquiries: 08457 484950
Floodline: 0845 988 1188
AA traffic and weather information line: 09003 401 100

Day river flowed through our home

Don family recall night of disaster

SOUTH YORKSHIRE
Martin Slack

SITTING around the TV on Monday night, Steve Green and his family watched with trepidation as the River Don burst its banks and inundated parts of Sheffield.

They saw RAF Sea King helicopters airlifting people to safety and watched as water from the river flowed down streets in the city centre. They knew they could be next.

The River Don runs just yards from the back door of their semi-detached house in the village of Sprotborough, and their home was downstream from the destruction they were witnessing.

At 4.45am on Tuesday morning, Mr Green, his wife, twin teenage sons and 21 year-old daughter, who is 32 weeks pregnant with her first child, were woken by the police who advised them to leave.

All they could do was move as many of their belongings upstairs as possible and then hope the floods did not sweep away too much of their lives.

Mr Green, 47, said: "It was not a big surprise when the police came banging on the door, but we didn't expect it to be as bad as it was. By 9am the water was rising quickly.

"We managed to get a lot of our gear upstairs, but things like carpets, settees and chairs are just completely ruined. The river was actually flowing through the downstairs of our house.

"I have lived here for 22 years and nothing like this has ever happened, but as the years have gone by the water has got closer every year when we have had a lot of rain."

Now the family face a long wait for an insurance assessor to come and survey the damage and Mr Green, who works in the building trade, said he hoped they were home in time to welcome his new grandchild.

A couple of miles further downstream, an Army Chinook helicopter was called in to lift huge bags of aggregate into place to shore up the banks of the Don.

Firefighters also mounted a huge search after reports that a man had fallen into Tiltshill Drain, a dyke in the Toll Bar area of Doncaster, but last night there was no evidence of any victim.

Drivers of Stagecoach buses in Doncaster found themselves ferrying hundreds of evacuees from their homes in the Bentley, Arksey and Almholme areas.

The buses themselves had to be moved from their depot close to the river on Tuesday night as floodwaters rose and the Mayor of Doncaster, Martin Winter, paid tribute to the firm, its drivers and others who had helped in the effort.

Elsewhere in the county, Barnsley Council said it had removed 500 tonnes of flood debris from streets across the borough and education officials and Hillsborough College in Sheffield would be closed until at least July 6 due to flood damage.

Sheffield City Council asked people who wanted to help those affected by the floods to send donations to the Lord Mayor's Fund – Flood, Lord Mayor's Office, Town Hall, Sheffield, S1 2HH. martin.slack@ypn.co.uk

Catastrophic: A resident leaves her house as floodwaters rise in Toll Bar, near Doncaster, yesterday. Forecasters say more rain is on the way.   Picture, Lewis Whyld/PA Wire

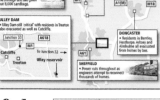

Washout: Flooding at the huge Meadowhall shopping centre in Sheffield, which has forced its closure.

Supplies to be cut as power is shared

Paul Whitehouse

MANY householders face days of planned power cuts in Sheffield because floods have damaged so much major equipment suppliers cannot get enough electricity into the city to meet demand.

A total of 48,000 customers were left without any power in South Yorkshire after the floods hit the region on Monday, with 76,000 of those in Sheffield and although electricity has since been restored to more than 67,000 of those affected, enforced cuts are being imposed because of supply problems.

In Sheffield and Hull areas, 7,500 customers were still without power last night while electricity had been restored to 78,000 properties.

The storms caused problems with both National Grid equipment and that operated by CE Electric UK, the regional electricity distributor, meaning too little electricity available to meet demand.

The company says that as it puts more customers back on line, the demand they make will exceed supply and there is no option but to impose structured power cuts, which will affect the city centre and some surrounding suburbs.

A CE Electric spokesman said: "We will need to start to limit the power being used throughout the day by imposing a series of relatively short, planned power cuts.

"Unfortunately, due to the number of important sites that have been affected, it is going to take several days before our customers' supplies are fully back to normal.

"We are working closely with our colleagues at National Grid, who have also suffered substantial damage to one of their main in feeds, to secure supplies in Sheffield."

SOUTH YORKSHIRE ON FLOOD ALERT   Graphic: Graeme Bandeira

BARNSLEY
● Council says it has had to clear 500 tonnes of flood debris from across the borough and has given out 8,000 sandbags.

ROAD CLOSED
● A61 between Sheffield and Barnsley closed southbound after it washed away.

ULLEY DAM
● Ulley Dam still 'critical' with residents in Treeton also evacuated as well as Catcliffe.

DONCASTER
● Residents in Bentley, Hexthorpe, Arksey and Almholme all evacuated from homes by bus.

SHEFFIELD
● Power cuts throughout as engineers attempt to reconnect thousands of homes.

Junction 33   A618   M1   To Junction 32   A61   Catcliffe   Treeton   Ulley reservoir

M1 reopens as dam-wall fears fade

ULLEY RESERVOIR
Paul Whitehouse
and Martin Slack

POLICE reopened the M1 near Sheffield last night after fears over the collapse of a nearby dam wall began to diminish.

Engineers said there was still a danger that Ulley reservoir could flood but added that a combined repair and pumping operation meant it was safe to open the motorway.

Residents from the villages of Whiston, Treeton and Catcliffe were moved out of their homes in the early hours of Tuesday because the dam was showing signs of weakening.

Those communities would be in the direct path of a wall of water if the dam burst and the M1 was closed because the carriageway would also be flooded.

But yesterday a police spokesman said it had been decided to allow traffic back on to the motorway despite the fact that work was continuing to make the dam safe.

Commuters travelling out of Sheffield and Rotherham last night still had to find alternative routes, because junction 32 and a large stretch of the A630 Sheffield Parkway remained closed.

The southbound carriageway was also restricted to two lanes and the southbound entry slip road at junction 34 at Meadowhall was also blocked off.

Firefighters from across the country were brought in to help with an operation to pump water out of Ulley reservoir to take pressure off the wall. They have been moving 6.5 million litres per hour.

That has reduced the water level by 75cm, but last night a fire service spokesman said a drop of at least two metres would be required to allow permanent repairs to the dam to take place.

The pumping operation was continuing last night and residents remained away from their homes, either staying with relatives or at an emergency accommodation centre set up at Dinnington Comprehensive School.

Jim Claydon, the engineer overseeing the repair operation, said 3,000 tonnes of stone was being used to shore up the structure. He added: "If the dam did fail, we are not going to see a tsunami-style wave sweeping down the valley. It would be a much more gradual release of water."

A third of all the high volume pumps available in the UK were in use at the site, but the fire service equipment is expected to be replaced by the private sector to allow firefighters to return to normal duties.

The closure of the M1 has caused serious traffic problems, with 15-mile tailbacks reported as a result.

Safe to return: The first vehicles move southbound on the M1 after the motorway was reopened last night.   Picture Chris Lawton.

Ford victim was county court judge

NATIONAL

A MOTORIST swept to his death as he tried to cross a flooded ford was a county court judge.

Eric Dickinson, 66, who sat in county courts across the West Midlands for more than 20 years, was found dead in his submerged car near Pershore, Worcestershire, on Tuesday evening.

A search was launched after Mr Dickinson rang his wife during Monday's heavy rain to tell her his Volvo was being overwhelmed by floodwaters.

Judge Dickinson, a former solicitor who lived in the Worcestershire village of Leigh for more than 30 years, leaves a widow, Gill, sons William and Mark, daughter Emma and six grandchildren.

His elder son William, who lives in Nottingham, said: "He was a very popular man with a good sense of humour. He was well known for the way in which he was able to defuse tense situations in court between opposite parties using humour and pathos while maintaining everyone's dignity.

"Away from his legal work, he never had any spare time because of his involvement in family, Rotary, the church and other interests. He gave his time unselfishly to other people."

The position in Lincolnshire, where dozens of people had been forced our of their homes by rising flood water, improved yesterday.

In Lincoln itself, the banks of the River Till burst overnight on Tuesday, flooding nearby Tillbridge Lane and closing several roads.

Heavy floods across the East Midlands may also have claimed the life of a 41-year-old Lincolnshire man. His body was found floating in the River Leen, in the Lenton area of Nottingham, at around 6.30pm on Monday.

The floods

FOR INFORMATION AND HELP
National Rail Inquiries: 08457 484950
Floodline: 0845 988 1188
AA traffic and weather information line: 09003 401 100

Angry residents turn on officials

Agency is accused of failures on drainage

Alexandra Wood

THE ENVIRONMENT Agency was accused yesterday of failing to maintain drains after thousands of residents in an East Yorkshire town were put on alert for more floods.

People living in Hedon were told to turn off their gas and electricity, move valuables out of harm's way and make sure there were sandbags outside properties as the agency issued a severe flood warning.

But representatives of internal drainage boards in the area said that they had been warning the agency for over a decade about the lack of maintenance on the land drains, which take water from agricultural land in Holderness to the Humber estuary.

The alert was issued after the Burstwick Drain overtopped, leading to flooding at the main A1033 road at Thorngumbald.

Yesterday afternoon police issued an appeal for people not to panic after a local college closed early to allow students to get home "in case of a worsening situation."

Ralph Ward, clerk to the Keyingham and Thorngumbald Internal Drainage Boards said various boards had been warning the agency about the need to regularly de-silt the tidal outfalls into the estuary. Some work had been done latterly, but over a long period they hadn't been maintained, he said.

"They need to have a proper maintenance programme for Hedon Haven and Stone Creek.

"There are places along the main drain which people have turned into gardens and obviously there haven't been people (from the agency) through for many years."

However a spokesman for the Environment Agency said it did regularly desilt the drain and backed up tidal flows to flush it out.

He added: "We will be talking to the Internal Drainage Boards in the near future to discuss where they believe the problem lies.

"However we had four inches of rain in twelve hours in that area recently, one sixth of the annual average, and this would cause problems for any area."

Throughout yesterday firefighters continued to pump away vast amounts of water which have kept streets in the Inmans area of Hedon under water since Monday.

Two high-volume pumps were at work off Greville Road, each pumping water at 7,000 litres per minute into Burstwick Drain, and another four were pumping water from Hedon Haven into the estuary.

The sluice gates into the estuary close at high tide and the pumps are vital to keep the water in the drain from building up.

In the town anger was growing about inadequate drainage with many people blaming new housing for overloading the system. Hedon has doubled in size in the last decade and much of the new development is close to the drain, at the south of the town.

There was also frustration that the Environment Agency is rethinking plans announced in January for an £800,000 pumping station.

In still flooded Brevere Road, one resident said it had been the fourth time there had been flooding in the area since 2000, adding: "The monks dug these drains – maybe it's time to dig another one. They will say it's the weather – I agree it's the weather – but why weren't we prepared?"

Retired joiner Jim Uney, 75, said he'd be calling for the removal of the area head of the Environment Agency at a meeting tonight.

"They have known about this for seven years. The time for waffle has finished. They should have uprated the pumping system. Bigger and better pumps should have been installed on Hedon Haven and Burstwick Drain.

"The residents are sick as hell of lame excuses."

The Environment Agency spokesman said it had done more work on the pumping station scheme – and it would not solve the problem. It is now considering raising the flood banks on the drain to protect residents in Burstwick and "at other appropriate places"

No entry: Police close the main road between Hull and Withernsea yesterday after flooding at Thorngumbald and a 'severe flood warning' at Hedon. Picture: Terry Carrott

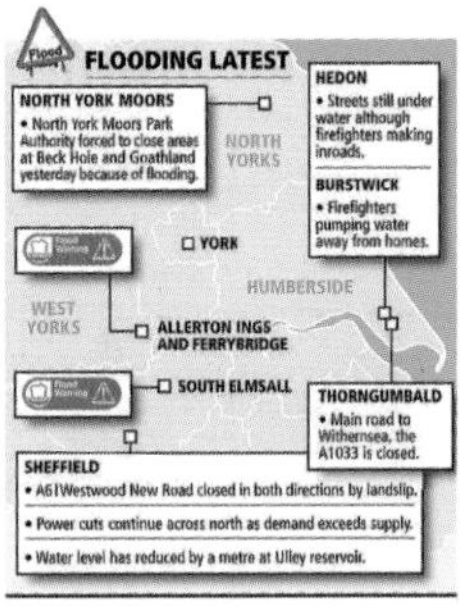
FLOODING LATEST
NORTH YORK MOORS
• North York Moors Park Authority forced to close areas at Beck Hole and Goathland yesterday because of flooding.
NORTH YORKS
HEDON
• Streets still under water although firefighters making inroads.
BURSTWICK
• Firefighters pumping water away from homes.
YORK
HUMBERSIDE
WEST YORKS
ALLERTON INGS AND FERRYBRIDGE
SOUTH ELMSALL
THORNGUMBALD
• Main road to Withernsea, the A1033 is closed.
SHEFFIELD
• A61Westwood New Road closed in both directions by landslip.
• Power cuts continue across north as demand exceeds supply.
• Water level has reduced by a metre at Ulley reservoir.

I'm tired out but I'm not giving in...

EAST YORKSHIRE

Simon Bristow

WHILE bleary-eyed firefighters were packing up their pumping gear in Kingswood, one of Hull's worst-hit areas, residents in the East Riding village of Leven were still sloshing about their homes in a foot of filthy flood water yesterday.

The contrast could not have been greater.

A mood of cautious optimism was rising above the debris in the Hull suburb as the water that had disrupted lives and destroyed property either sank beneath the earth or was carried away by the River Hull.

Householders were full of praise for the firecrews who had worked around the clock to clear the area, pumping 24,000 litres a minute along mile-long yellow pipes into the river, which threatened but ultimately resisted the urge to burst its banks and render their efforts useless.

Some felt they had even benefited from the experience.

Alma Morris, an 80-year-old resident of Sovereign Way, was looking on the bright side as she brushed twigs, litter and worse from her drive.

She said: "I'm tired out but I'm not giving in. It was horrendous. It only flooded my porch but I was marooned and on my own, even though my daughter lives across the street.

"But the community spirit has been tremendous. I've lived here four years and didn't really know my neighbours but they were wonderful. They kept coming to ask me if I was all right and the people across the road sent me two pints of milk and I've never spoken to them before.

"It shows what you can do when you stick together."

Mrs Morris, like scores of others across the region, had been evacuated during the height of the crisis and was beginning to restore a semblance of normality to her home.

Others are less fortunate.

In the Cooper's Croft area of Leven, stoicism was giving way to anger as residents began to feel abandoned.

Ian Stones celebrated his 46th birthday yesterday facing another night away from home with wife Jane, 44, 20-year-old daughter Amy and son Joshua, 16.

He said the two pumps supposed to alleviate the flood, belonging to builders Scrutons, had not been in action since Monday night.

He said: "One is for the rain water and the other is to take sewage away, but they packed up because the electrics to run them are under three feet of water.

"We are now getting some of the waste coming back, it's not very pleasant. The water has gone down but it's still at the height of the first stair and there are about 40 houses down the street affected.

"We know other people have had it much worse but we could be in rented accommodation for months."

Residents and the emergency services are bracing themselves for another downpour at the weekend.

Christine Randall, deputy leader of Hull Council, said the authority hoped to have 10,000 sandbags ready for distribution tonight.

She said: "We will be as well prepared as we possibly can. All non-essential council business has been cancelled. The priority is to reduce the risk to life. We have learned from what happened on Monday and we will decide where the pinch points are and respond as quickly as we can to any serious flooding."

You have nothing to fear from looters, police assure evacuees

SOUTH YORKSHIRE

Paul Whitehouse

PRIVATE security guards have been drafted in to help police protect communities abandoned in the Sheffield floods although the force has reported a "significant" reduction in crime since the waters overwhelmed the city.

Assistant Chief Constable Mark Whyman said there had been many "wild rumours" circulating about looting since the chaos began but insisted: "I really want to dispel those"

So far police have had no reports of crimes which could be attributed to looting, though he added the full situation would only become clear when residents forced out by flood water were finally allowed to return to their homes.

"There will be the odd rogue out to take advantage, but we will be watching for them," he said, adding that although numbers of calls to the force had increased over the last few days, numbers of crime reports had dropped.

Protecting people's property had been "built into" plans he said, with extra patrols working in the areas affected and the council deploying their own housing security guards to provide added protection.

"South Yorkshire is a safe place to live and we are making it as safe as we can for people who have to leave their properties," he said.

Deeply disturbing: The delivery of sandbags to the village of Bentley near Doncaster, South Yorkshire, where the flood level has risen overnight.

The county had suffered a lot of damage to its infrastructure and it would take time for that to be repaired.

He has been the police 'gold' commander, in charge of the operation for the last few days and has been holding regular briefings with other agencies, including councils and those from transport bodies and power companies, to monitor progress and assess priorities.

"My message is that we need to be patient. It will be a long road to recovery. Some roads have structural problems which will take some time to repair," he said.

Those highways include the A61 near High Green, where the carriageway was ripped apart as water apparently shifted the land beneath it.

Although it is one of the city's major routes, it is expected to remain closed for several more days until the surface can be restored.

That is among six roads in the county which remain closed, and others are still only passable with care. In addition, many roads now open have been left with potholes or other carriageway damage which will need expensive repairs.

Around 350 people were in emergency evacuation centres in Doncaster yesterday after being evacuated from homes in Bentley, Toll Bar and Arksey after the River Don burst its banks.

The danger at Ulley reservoir in Rotherham has now largely passed, with the water level reduced by a metre and thousands of tonnes of stone used to shore up the dam wall where it had started to crumble.

It was expected that residents evacuated as a safety precaution in the villages of Whiston, Treeton and Catcliffe, will shortly be allowed home.

Planning meetings have also been held to start making arrangements to rehouse residents in areas like Catcliffe and Toll Bar, Doncaster, where homes have been so badly affected by flooding they will need extensive work to make them habitable.

In Barnsley more than 500 homes have been affected, with the council offering help to both its own tenants and private householders, moving 650 tonnes of debris and ruined furniture and also carrying out safety checks on gas and electricity supplies.

The authority is also offering assistance to those who need it, because officials have discovered severe hardship among those who have no insurance or have experienced delays in processing claims.

Council Leader Steve Houghton said: "The Council is concerned over the high levels of hardship being suffered.

"We are providing a package of measures to make sure homes are safe, flood debris is removed, health advice is available, and that the most vulnerable homes have basic amenities in place as quickly as possible."

Sandbags at the ready as more rain expected

WEST YORKSHIRE

Joanne Ginley

THE clean-up was continuing as officials drew up plans to cope with further rainfall predicted for this weekend.

Yesterday in South Elmsall and Agbrigg, near Wakefield, a general clean-up operation was taking place. In Agbrigg the weather conditions left some without power but it was hoped supplies would be restored.

Flood warnings remained in place at several locations across West Yorkshire including the River Aire at Allerton Ings, South Elmsall and the Aire at Ferrybridge.

Yesterday Malcolm Wilcox, emergency planning manager for Wakefield Council, said that following warnings of more rain on Saturday and Sunday preparation work was under way.

"We will have a further 11,500 sandbags ready by then and we will store them where we have identified vulnerable areas so we can get them to people as quickly as possible. We are clearing drains, clearing culverts and checking and clearing screens on watercourses. We have staff on standby all weekend and are doing everything we can that might help alleviate any flooding."

Sandal and Agbrigg Community Centre will be open all weekend if people need help. Parts of Leeds have also been hit hard, with homes flooded in areas including the Dunhills estate in east Leeds, Collingham, near Wetherby, and Kippax.

A spokeswoman for Leeds City Council said meetings had taken place to ensure the city could cope if bad weather hit again. Staff have been put on standby, arrangements are in place to deal with vulnerable people at risk and council liaison staff have been out in the affected communities giving support and advice.

Monday's floods hit many areas including Mirfield, Liversedge, Wakefield, Cleckheaton, Brighouse, Pontefract and Castleford.

TRAVEL CHAOS

Roads closed last night

- A616 – Pleasly Road, Aughton
- A61 – Westwood New Road, Burn Cross
- A633 – Station Road, Wath Upon Dearn
- A6023 – Waith Road, Swinton
- A630 – Centenary Way, Rotherham
- A6102 – Middlewood Road, North Sheffield
- A631 – Bawtry Road, Rotherham
- A631 – Gainsborough Road, Bawtry
- A631 – Bawtry Road, Tickhill
- A19 – Doncaster Road, Toll Bar
- A6123 – Aldwark Lane, Rotherham

Train Disruption

- Transpennine Express service from Liverpool to York has reopened with one train per hour operating in each direction calling additionally at Bradford Interchange and Halifax.
- A shuttle service is running between Manchester Piccadilly and Huddersfield once an hour in each direction.
- Shuttle services will also operate once an hour in each direction between Leeds and Hull, York and Scarborough, York to Middlesborough, York and Newcastle, Manchester Airport and Sheffield and Scunthorpe to Cleethorpes.
- A bus replacement will run between Scunthorpe and Doncaster.
- GNER is operating as normal between London, King's Cross and York.
- Hourly services will operate between London and Leeds with replacement coaches between Wakefield and Doncaster.
- There will be no GNER services between Harrogate, Bradford, Skipton or Hull.
- Midland Mainline is running its published timetable for all routes, with the exception of Doncaster and Barnsley.
- Services for Leeds will run but not stop at Doncaster.
- Barnsley services will start and terminate at Sheffield.
- Virgin services are running as normal.

Emergency services are ready for more challenges after busy week

NORTH YORKSHIRE

Paul Jeeves

OFF-DUTY staff from North Yorkshire's fire brigade have been put on alert to deal with another wave of flooding disasters as more downpours are predicted for the weekend.

An internal memo has been circulated by senior officers from North Yorkshire Fire and Rescue Service to inform staff that they may need to be called back on duty for more emergency call-outs.

The North Yorkshire brigade witnessed what is thought to have been its busiest 24-hour period in living memory at the start of the week as crews and support staff battled to deal with hundreds of calls.

During Monday night alone, firefighters responded to more than 200 calls and dealt with flooding in over 400 premises.

More heavy rain has been predicted over the weekend, with forecasters claiming the worst downpours are expected on Saturday.

The North Yorkshire fire brigade's station manager, Carl Boasman, said: "Up until now we have coped very well, and this is down to the efforts of all our staff.

"We are working closely with the Environment Agency to identify any problem areas, but it is very difficult to predict. We do expect problems with heavy rainfall, especially with the amount of water that is already in watercourses and in the ground."

The clean-up operation was continuing yesterday across the region, including Scarborough, Pickering and Selby.

Pumps were used throughout Wednesday night and yesterday to prevent flooding in the Scarborough Road area of Norton-on Derwent, as well as Old Malton.

A Ryedale District Council spokeswoman stressed that routes into Pickering had now fully re-opened after the A169 and A170 were closed earlier this week.

Despite the flood waters abating in North Yorkshire, another two areas, near Beck Hole and Goathland, had to be closed to the public by the North York Moors National Park Authority.

A performing arts festival which was due to be held in Rowntree Park in York on Sunday has been cancelled and York Council also warned residents that sandbags will not be available for personal use from the authority's EcoDepot in Hazel Court off James Street so they could be used in the areas most at risk of flooding

GIVE YOUR SUPPORT

- **South Yorkshire flood fund:** Being run by South Yorkshire Community Foundation – to donate visit www.justgiving.com/southyorkshirefloodrelief or pay cash into Yorkshire Bank through sort code 05-08-03 account number 21890701
- **Sheffield Council:** To make a donation send cheques, made payable to Sheffield Council's Lord Mayor's Charity – Flood Fund, to The Lord Mayor's Charity – Flood, Lord Mayor's Office, Town Hall, Sheffield, S1 2HH.
- **Hallam FM flood victim support appeal:** To donate to this appeal, make your cheque payable to South Yorkshire Flood Victim Support Appeal, and pay it in at any branch of the Yorkshire Bank.

(bottom) **Deeply disturbing:** The delivery of sandbags to the village of Bentley near Doncaster, South Yorkshire, on June 28, where the flood level rose overnight.

www.yorkshirepost.co.uk　　　　　　　　　　YORKSHIRE POST FRIDAY JUNE 29 2007　9

The floods

FOR INFORMATION AND HELP
National Rail Inquiries: 08457 484950
Floodline: 0845 988 1188
AA traffic and weather information line: 09003 401 100

Clean-up operation in progress: What was the flood-ravaged centre of Catcliffe, Rotherham, is, right, now being brought back to normal with the aid of heavy equipment.　　Pictures: Chris Lawton

'It's all ruined and the worst is council cannot pay us out'

Martin Slack

AS dawn broke over the flood-ravaged village of Catcliffe, Rotherham, yesterday an eerie silence still hung over the houses which had been inundated with seven or eight feet of water.

Cars left behind were covered with a film of mud and a water line on the walls of homes showed exactly how high the floodwater had been before receding.

Householders were still at refuge centres in schools or were staying with friends and relatives, unsure of when they would be able to return after three nights away.

But as fears faded over a burst at the nearby Ulley dam some of the more adventurous residents began to bring life back to the streets and faced the horrendous task of cleaning up.

Dennis and Jeanette Dryden had just finished getting their bungalow, at the corner of Frederick Street and Sheffield Lane, exactly how they wanted it after spending around £10,000.

When they left early on Tuesday they had no time to pick up any of their possessions, even leaving their beloved budgie Tommy behind in his cage in the lounge.

The bird survived but the rest of the couple's world was literally turned upside down by the deluge, with the TV set lying face down on the soggy hearth rug.

Breaking down in tears as she surveyed the chaos, Mrs Dryden, 47, said: "Every thing is ruined and the worst thing is we have been told by the council that we are not insured.

"We have spent thousands of our own money on this bungalow, which is owned by the council, and we have been paying a premium with our rent but they say they can't pay out.

"When the police came round in the middle of the night they just told us we had to get out – we didn't have time to move anything. All we had were the clothes we were stood up in.

"Now I am wearing my sister-in-law's clothes and all mine are completely ruined. I had just bought a cocktail dress for a party, which cost

POWER BACK – WITH A WARNING

Power lost because of the floods was restored to over 8,000 properties last night, but there were safety warnings to people returning home.

The numbers without electricity in South Yorkshire yesterday fell from 86,000 to under 1,000. Controlled power cuts continued there last night to allow power sharing at peak times. in Hull and North Lincolnshire 150 of the 10,000 customers affected by the storms were still without power.

Regional distributor CE Electric UK warned people returning to flooded properties of possible hazards caused by water damage to wiring and said they should arrange an inspection by a qualified electrical contractor.

hundreds. It's wrecked along with everything else." Mr Dryden, 67, told how the water slowly rose towards their home during Monday but added it was pumped away until the fire service was called to deal with the Ulley dam crisis.

He said: "We went to bed on Monday night and thought it would be all right but the water just kept coming.

"At about 4am the police came and told us to get out. We went to Dinnington School and then our family came and picked us up. We have been there since."

Down the street in Orgreave Road, Mike Torr and his fiancee Nadine Russell were coming to terms with the fact that they would not be moving back into their home until after they were married in October.

Mr Torr, 23, a liaison officer said: "In the previous heavy rain on June 15. the road flooded and we had a meeting with Rotherham Council about our worries. They said we wouldn't flood but we did." Miss Russell, 25, who runs a home beauty therapy business, has lost money because she couldn't work and was worried about the threat of looters in the unoccupied homes.

She said: "Monday night was terrifying. We had to wade out of the house waist deep in water and get in a boat which took us to dry land. Then we got on a bus and went to Herringthorpe Leisure Centre... When we came back this morning it was horrible. Everything has floated around in the downstairs of the house and it will take at least six months before we can move back in."

martin.slack@ypn.co.uk

WEATHER WATCH

Next four days in Yorkshire:

TODAY	Light showers	
SATURDAY	Heavy rain	
SUNDAY	Heavy showers	
MONDAY	Heavy showers	

Surveying the damage: Jeanette and Dennis Dryden had spent about £10,000 getting their bungalow at Catcliffe exactly as they wanted it.

Hunt for a modest Superman in river rescue bid

Paul Whitehouse

A "TRUE hero" who dived into fast-flowing water to rescue an elderly flood victim was being sought by police last night, because he slipped away from the scene as emergency services arrived.

He was described as acting like Superman during the incident where he hauled Peter Harding, 68, from the torrent of water beneath a railway bridge in Newhall Road in the the Lower Don Valley, Sheffield, on Monday evening as the area was engulfed by flood water from the river.

Mr Harding did not survive the incident after being swept from his feet, but officers want to trace the man who pulled him from the water.

Speaking at the scene of the tragedy, Chief Supt Jon House described how the stranger came across a group of people struggling under the bridge.

He calmly took off his coat and handed it to an onlooker before diving straight in to the deep, fast-flowing water.

Then he conducted what appeared to be a professional underwater search, before dragging Mr Harding out of the water and starting work to revive him.

But Mr House said that when paramedics arrived and took control the man took his camouflage jacket back and walked off.

How officers are trying to trace him, not only so he can help with the coroner's investigation, but so Mr Harding's family can thank him.

Mr House said: "As the River Don flooded the water came straight along here where the road dips under the bridge.

"As a result of this several members of the public grabbed hold of girders to save their lives.

"They looked round and saw him (Mr Harding) and he slipped down underneath the water."

Mr House said the people clinging to the metal girders beneath the bridge shouted to the man they want to trace who was approaching the scene.

"This hero appeared from nowhere," he said.

"He, just like Superman, took off his jacket and gave it to another member of the public.

"He said 'hold on to that, keep it dry' and dived straight into the water."

Mr House said the mystery hero is a white man in his 30s.

Rescuers' kit gets clean-up

Laundry load: West Yorkshire fireman Ian Thompson among uniforms to be cleaned. Picture: Gary Longbottom

IT IS not only homes, businesses and streets throughout West Yorkshire that need a clean following this week's floods.

Yesterday over 200 sets of firefighting kit used in flood relief work over the last few days across the county had to be shipped off for professional cleaning from West Yorkshire Fire and Rescue Service's base in Birkenshaw.

In the 15 hours to midnight on Monday, West Yorkshire fire crews responded to about 1,600 calls to flooding, 20 incidents involving rescues.

Two elderly people were rescued by firefighters using a water sled in Mexwrood, Leeds; two adults and four children were plucked from a minibus in Gomersal; and several streets had to be evacuated in the Agbrigg area of Wakefield.

(top two pictures): Clean-up operation in progress: What was the flood ravaged centre of Catcliffe, Rotherham, was, on June 28 being brought back to normal with the aid of heavy equipment.

(directly below) Surveying the damage: Jeanette and Dennis Dryden had spent about £10,000 getting their bungalow at Catcliffe exactly as they wanted it.

The floods

FOR INFORMATION AND HELP
National Rail Inquiries: 08457 484950
Floodline: 0845 988 1188
AA traffic and weather information line: 09003 401 100

Stricken schools may face more disruption

Further heavy rain could delay plans to reopen

EAST YORKSHIRE

Simon Bristow

HUNDREDS of children in Hull and the East Riding are facing major disruption to their education as a result of flood damage to their schools.

With more heavy rain expected over the weekend, council officials in Hull concede there may be more to add to the list of nine schools already in danger of staying closed until September.

Sydney Smith in Anlaby is the worst-hit secondary school in the city, where 180 ground-floor rooms were still under 4ft of water yesterday. Headteacher Kevin Beaton said it would take until Easter 2008 for repairs to be completed.

The most severely affected primary schools are Rokeby Park, Westcott, Tilbury, Bude Park, Sutton Park, St James, Thorpepark and Ganton Special School.

Council leader Carl Minns said it was hoped pupils could be accommodated at other schools or other facilities, but it was too early to give details.

He said: "As it stands some schools will not open again this term, but what makes it difficult to plan is the threat of more flooding this weekend.

"I want to get on and sort this out but we need to get through the next few days first. The priority then will be working out what we do for the next two weeks."

East Riding Council said it was confident of accommodating children from flood-hit primary schools Anlaby Acre Heads, Cottingham Croxby, Hedon Inmans, and St Mary and St Joseph's, in Pocklington, in other schools.

In Hedon, where Thursday night's severe flood warning had been downgraded yesterday, Humberside Fire and Rescue Service and the Environment Agency were still working hard to clear the streets of flood water.

A huge Environment Agency pump arrived in the town at lunchtime. By 6pm it was expected to be pumping 1,320 gallons a minute into Hedon Haven.

Six other pumps operated by agency staff and the fire brigade were removing a similar volume at the same rate at the sluice gates.

"We'll be here as long as we are needed," was the reassuring message from Allen Cunningham, the brigade's community safety manager.

In Hull, 10,000 homes have been flooded. More than 1,000 residential properties and 300 businesses were hit across the East Riding, while in north-east Lincolnshire the toll was 500 homes and 80 commercial properties.

Authorities across the region were preparing a stockpile of sandbags to minimise the effect of any further flooding this weekend.

In response to the concerns of many evacuated residents, vital impact was uppermost in the minds of residents in Sorrel Drive in Hull.

With the potential for more damage, the final bill for the clean-up operation can still only be guessed at.

Concern about the financial impact was apparent in the minds of residents in Sorrel Drive in Hull.

The normally neat-looking new estate more closely resembled a refugee camp when the waters had subsided, with furniture and clothing being left out in the street to dry.

Karen Mortensen, who spent £105 on a hotel room on Monday night, said: "You wonder who will insure you after this. Some people are already saying it might knock £30,000 off the value of their houses."

zimon.bristow@ypn.co.uk

Clearing up: Water is pumped from Hedon into Burstwick Drain. Picture: Terry Carrott.

Flotsam: Two cars now seen in the middle of the swollen River Don at Meadow Hall Road, Sheffield, following the floods. Picture: Chris Lawton.

Mayor claims town 'let down' in crisis

SOUTH YORKSHIRE

Martin Slack

AS hundreds of people faced up to their flood nightmares yesterday, Mayor of Doncaster Martin Winter said he felt that the emergency response system had "failed" people in the town.

Sheffield, Rotherham and Barnsley were recovering from the effects of Monday's rain but some areas of Doncaster were still being pumped out, with about 300 people in refuge centres.

Mr Winter spent several hours in Bentley and Toll Bar, the neighbourhoods hit hardest, travelling by boat to meet people who were trying to come to terms with what had happened to them.

But he said he felt that communities in Doncaster, which is downstream of Sheffield and took longer to bear the brunt of the rain, had been "unable to access the resources they needed".

He said: "I feel that, as mayor, I should have been making a much stronger case to those directing the emergency services and that they should have been sending more resources into these communities.

"I feel personally that we have let them down. I understand that Ukay was the priority, but these people have been left alone to bear the disasters in their own communities. We couldn't get pumps in here to take the water away."

Mr Winter added that he had travelled around the area people had been angry at the response and had spoken to him about their frustration with the system.

But a spokesman for South Yorkshire Police said senior officers, who had chaired the response command, did not accept that the emergency services had treated the Doncaster area differently.

The spokesman said: "Our focus, as it has been throughout, is on looking after all the people affected by flooding across the county. No requests from Doncaster have been refused by any members of the Gold control centre, which includes fire, military and other services, as well as a representative of Doncaster Council.

"It is a matter of regret that despite an open invitation Mayor Winter has never attended Gold centre, unlike the chief executives of the other boroughs affected.

"We understand that he has only visited the Silver control in Doncaster once and then only briefly, so it may be that he doesn't fully understand the situation."

Yesterday South Yorkshire Fire and Rescue deployed most of its high volume pumps to the Bentley and Toll Bar areas and chief fire officer Mark Smitherman admitted the Ulley dam had been "a major pull on resources".

Meanwhile police, the Environment Agency (EA), and council and health workers continued to work around the clock to help evacuees.

With more wet weather expected, the Ea Beck at Toll Bar last night remained the subject of a severe flood warning – the EA's most serious flood alert.

Severe flood warnings also remained in place at four points on the River Don – at Bentley, Bentley Moor, Willow Bridge caravan site and the areas of Thorpe in Balne, Kirk Bramwith, Braithwaite and Trumfleet.

As a precaution Kirk Bramwith and Braithwaite residents have been told to be prepared to evacuate their properties. Nearby Arksey and Almholme are also at risk.

● The effects of the floods in South Yorkshire will be studied as part of a £2.5m research project of the Catchment Science Centre, run by Sheffield University and the EA, looking at future development on the River Don flood plain.

Region's death toll rises following canal plunge

Martin Slack and Jenni Marsh

POLICE yesterday revealed that floodwaters had claimed another victim in the region after a man from a village near Doncaster fell into a swollen canal.

The 60-year-old, who has not yet been named by police, is understood to be from Walberingham, east of Doncaster, and was found in the Foxlyn Canal, in Tockey, Lincolnshire.

It is understood that the victim fell from a dinghy near the village's Elms Retirement Park, in Main Street. Police were called at about 10am on Thursday and the body was found three hours later.

An RAF rescue helicopter and the Lincolnshire and Nottinghamshire air ambulance was drafted in for the search and thermal imaging equipment was used to try to find the man, who was eventually located near his boat.

Coroner Roger Atkinson is expected to open an inquest next week.

At the ready: Workers build a wall from sandbags outside Meadowhall shopping centre, Sheffield, to prevent further flooding this weekend. Staff were working towards reopening on Monday. Picture: John Nguyen/Terri Parry Agency.

Drainage ditches 'played role in drenching'

Chris Benfield

UPLAND drainage ditches, dug by farmers at a cost of millions of man-hours and huge subsidies over the second half of the 20th century, are suspected of contributing to the flooding which hit the lowlands this week.

Several schemes to fill the ditches in again are now in progress, at more cost to the taxpayer.

A scientist who has looked into the history of flooding in Yorkshire says there is no doubt that Leeds and York suffered less when the catchment areas of the Aire and the Ouse were in their natural state, before the post-war drive to turn peat bog into grazing land.

And accelerated run-off from the Peak District moors, where the original drains have been eroded into huge gullies, may have contributed to Sheffield's suffering this week.

The Environment Agency was alerted to the problem in 2004, in a report from its North East Fisheries Ecology and Recreation Advisory Committee. The committee was concerned about a number of consequences of the drains known to farmers as "grips".

The water running through them was washing away peat and affecting wildlife in the rivers it ran into. The drying of the peat was releasing stored carbon into the atmosphere, in the form of the greenhouse gas CO2. And it seemed likely that rivers would be filling up faster than natural if less rain was held in upland "sponges".

The chairman of the committee at the time was a Durham landowner, Hugh Becker of Barnard Castle.

He said yesterday: "It's a matter of simple logic that if you remove some of the soil's capacity to absorb and retain water, you are going to change the timing of flood peaks in the rivers."

Government bodies are now sponsoring experiments in filling the ditches and trying to measure the difference that makes.

Leeds University geographer Joe Holden, who is monitoring a number of peatland repair schemes, said: "The impact of the grips depends on where they are, of course, but we can say that places like Leeds and York have flooded more frequently since the 1960s than they did before and it is not all explained by rainfall."

chris.benfield@ypn.co.uk

GIVE YOUR SUPPORT

■ **South Yorkshire flood fund:** Being run by South Yorkshire Community Foundation – to donate visit www.justgiving.com/southyorkshirefloodrelief or pay cash into Yorkshire Bank through sort code 05-08-03, account number 21890701

■ **Sheffield Council:** To make a donation send cheques, made payable to Sheffield Council's Lord Mayor's Charity – Flood Fund, to The Lord Mayor's Charity – Flood, Lord Mayor's Office, Town Hall, Sheffield, S1 2HH.

■ **Hull flood victim support appeal:** To donate to this appeal, make your cheque payable to South Holderness Flood Victim Support appeal and pay it in at any branch of the Yorkshire Bank.

Severe weather forces gala cancellation

WEST YORKSHIRE

Robert Sutcliffe and Jenni Marsh

THE extreme weather conditions have led to some of this weekend's events across West Yorkshire being cancelled.

Leeds Council said it was looking at a range of measures to combat the risk of more flooding and Northern Rail advised passengers not to travel unless it was vital to do so.

The council's measures include:

■ All relevant departments have been asked to ensure that adequate personnel are on stand-by.

■ Street cleansing teams are visiting known hot spots to reduce the risk of flooding through the unblocking of drains

■ Arrangements are in place to deal with vulnerable people at risk

■ Highways depots have replenished stocks of the necessary resources to respond.

■ All sandbags will not be collected until Monday at the earliest.

For the first time in its 40-year history the annual Brighouse Charity Gala had to go ahead today. Gala officials made the difficult decision after meeting in Wellholme Park.

Today's Race for Life event designed to raise money for Cancer Research UK, at Temple Newsam, Leeds, has had to be rearranged for July 28 and tomorrow's event has been postponed to July 29.

Rail passengers were given a warning yesterday by Northern Rail not to travel this weekend unless necessary.

A spokeswoman said: "Our services are all back to our mad, except South Yorkshire and Lincolnshire where there has been particularly bad weather.

"For the weekend we are not expecting adverse weather conditions – the flood warnings have been lowered and there is less rainfall predicted than was forecast earlier in the week.

"However, we would still advise those hoping to travel by train this weekend not to do so unless it is necessary as we cannot guarantee the weather forecast."

Fresh warnings on safety

NORTH YORKSHIRE

Mark Branagan

FIRE fighters are giving last-minute warnings to North Yorkshire residents as the county braces itself for more heavy rain over the weekend following the floods that swamped Pickering and parts of Selby.

"Children should not be allowed to play in flood water, which can become contaminated with sewage and chemicals Do not smoke, eat or drink whilst in contact with floodwater and always wash your hands afterwards."

A spokesman added: "Even shallow water moving fast can sweep you off your feet and there may be hidden dangers such as open drains, damaged road surfaces, submerged debris or deep channels; these can cause serious injuries or even death.

"Children should not be allowed to play in flood water, which can become contaminated with sewage and chemicals Do not smoke, eat or drink whilst in contact with floodwater and always wash your hands afterwards."

Residents are being urged to monitor weather reports on local TV and radio and not to venture out in heavy storms unless it is absolutely necessary.

There is also an appeal for residents to look out for neighbours because people have been known to suffer from hypothermia after their homes have become flooded with cold rainwater even in summer.

I'm no hero says rescue-bid Superman

Tom Smithard

A MAN dubbed "Superman" for his attempts to resuscitate a pensioner killed in this week's floods said yesterday he was no hero.

He had been wading through Brightside Lane in Sheffield on Monday when he came across 68-year-old Peter Harding, who was struggling in fast-flowing water. The man, a 48-year-old named only as Darren, spoke to police yesterday after hearing he was a vital witness to the incident.

He said later: "I stripped off and went in the water. I tried to find him and luckily I saw the top of his head, grabbed him, then made my way back to the bank and gave him CPR until emergency services arrived.

"Peter didn't look his age. He looked younger than me, and I was living in hope that he'd made it through.

In hospital they told me he was very ill and that was the last I heard."

Chief Superintendent Jon House, said: "The fact that this gentleman doesn't want any fuss typifies his modest approach to attempting to save a man's life. This is just one example of the heroism and community spirit shown across South Yorkshire in these difficult times."

TRAVEL CHAOS

Roads closed last night

■ **Sheffield:** A61 Penistone Road at Crown Inn

■ **Rotherham:** The M1 motorway has now reopened. Access to the Parkway at Handsworth is closed. A6023 Rowms Lane, Swinton

■ **Doncaster:** A19 Askern

Road between Askern Road North of Toll Bar and A638 St Marys Roundabout.
A19 High Street, Bentley
A19 Bentley Road, Bentley
■ **East Riding:** A1033 between Hedon and Thorngumbald.

Train disruption

■ **Midland Mainline:** Services to Leeds will run as normal but will not stop at Doncaster.
■ **GNER:** An hourly service will operate between London and Leeds. All operators will operate between Wakefield and Doncaster.
■ No GNER services will operate from Harrogate, Bradford, Skipton or Hull.
■ **Northern Rail:** A two-hourly

service is operating on the Huddersfield – Barnsley line.
The following services are not running:
● Doncaster – Sheffield
● Doncaster – Scunthorpe
● Doncaster – Goole
● Doncaster – Leeds
● Northam Central Station
● Sheffield – Lincoln
But replacement services will operate on the above routes.

www.yorkshirepost.co.uk — YORKSHIRE POST WEDNESDAY JULY 4 2007 — 7

Floods The big clean-up

Sweeping clear: After the floods, the big clean up begins as the people of Bentley, near Doncaster, go back to their devastated shops and homes and clear the ruined stock and property onto the road for disposal.
Picture: John Giles/PA.

Families back to salvage lives after deluge

Anna Smith

A THICK sludge coats the carpets and wooden floor boards of Michelle and Stuart Birkby's home in Toll Bar, Doncaster.

In the living room, a dark water line runs the length of the walls and computer equipment, drawers and kitchen chairs lay strewn around the dining room, still wet with dirty flood water.

Life has come to a standstill for the Birkby's, along with dozens of families from the area, who were forced to flee their homes when floods ravaged the South Yorkshire village last Tuesday.

"It's been a nightmare. We were on holiday and had to return early. We couldn't believe it when we saw the damage. The water was as high as my waist," said Mrs Birkby, who lives on Askern Road with Stuart and son John, eight.

"It's what to do next that's worrying us. There's all the cleaning out and finding what we can salvage and what we can't. We were preparing to put the house on the market, but nobody's going to buy it now.

"Thankfully we were insured and have been offered alternative accommodation but I don't know when we will be back in the house."

Many properties in the village are still under water. Residents continue to shelter at a nearby leisure centre, desperately awaiting news about when it is safe to return to their homes and get their lives back on track.

Fellow flood victim Carl Harris returned to his water hit home for the first time yesterday to assess the damage and salvage the few possessions not destroyed.

The 32 year-old salesman returned to his property on Manor Estate, which is still knee-deep in dirty water, to find his fridge freezer floating in the living room alongside toys belonging to his five-year-old step-daughter Olivia.

Mr Harris, along with partner Cheryl, managed to hoist the three piece suite to safety on the kitchen work tops. But many of the family's possessions have been ruined, with the cost of replacements totalling thousands of pounds.

"Almost everything downstairs is wrecked and the water's still around 2ft deep. We're not insured and I'd say we are looking at a bill of £10,000 to £15,000.

"I don't know if or when we'll be going back home," he said.

Firefighters have been working around the clock to clear water from the village using 21 high volume pumps to move a million litres of water an hour into Ea Beck, which joins the River Don.

Fire chiefs reassured residents they would remain in the area for as long as they are needed to help to get the community back on its feet.

Station Manager Phil Shillito said: "Crews have worked tirelessly here and in all the other areas affected by flooding in South Yorkshire. There is still a lot of work to be done, but we are making good progress.

"Unfortunately it takes time to remove all the water from areas like this, but people have been patient and really got behind us."

The Prince of Wales was today expected to meet residents affected by the floods and give his support to the emergency services and volunteers. It will be his second visit to South Yorkshire in less than a week.

anna.smith@ypn.co.uk

'We are looking at a bill of £10,000 to £15,000. I don't know if or when we'll be going back home.'

Irreplaceable treasures washed away

Simon Bristow

IT is not the furniture, the carpets, the kitchen units or the newly-fitted blinds that Nevenka Peters frets over as she trudges around the empty shell of her modern, semi-detached house in Churchill Rise, Burstwick.

They, like the car and the TV, have gone.

But it is the family photographs and keepsakes, the things that made her house a home, that convey the real value of what she has lost.

"It's the things you can't replace that really bother you," she said.

"You hope you might have picked them up in the panic and put them somewhere safe, but until we get back to normal we just don't know.

"My neighbour has lost all her videos of her little ones. That's what you think about. It's soul-destroying."

Yet despite the devastation wreaked by the floods in this East Riding village, Mrs Peters still considers herself one of the lucky ones.

She watched with growing anxiety as the water rose inexorably up the garden towards her home from the street; a combination of blocked drains and flood water from the surrounding fields more than a match for the sandbags her husband Hamish had hastily deployed.

The couple, carrying two-and-a-half-year-old daughter Talia above their heads, waded through waist-deep water to reach the safety of her father's van. It is at his house in Station Road that they have been sheltering this past week – and they have no idea when their home will be habitable again.

Mrs Peters said: "I rang 999 but they just gave me a lot number. They didn't really give me any advice or help. They just said 'move everything upstairs and live upstairs', but I started worrying about my daughter. How could you live in a house like that?

"I rang my dad and told him to bring his waders. We're lucky he lives so near; some of the neighbours are paying £300 a night to live in a hotel."

The 31-year-old had returned to her property to let a restoration firm sent by her insurers carry out preliminary work.

She said the company was so busy in the area staff had been drafted in from Belfast.

Amid the upheaval is the need to keep Talia happy and keep her life as normal as possible.

Mrs Peters said: "She's doing extra days at nursery, which helps, but she asks what's going on and we've just told her the house is poorly. That's what she understands."

simon.bristow@ypn.co.uk

Clear-up: Nevenka Peters, above, clears her flooded home of a damaged TV, carpets and furniture in Churchill Rise, Burstwick, near Hull, more than a week after the storms devastated the area. Jane Rayworth, left, drags a ruined carpet from her flooded home in Churchill Rise, Burstwick.
Pictures: Terry Carrott.

Devastation: Michelle Birkby of Askern Road, Toll Bar, Doncaster, checks the damage to her flooded home after the flood receded.
Picture Chris Lawton.

Flash flood horror for villagers

Fiona Evans

FLASH floods in North Yorkshire brought desperate calls to the fire brigade yesterday evening.

Firefighters in the county said they had experienced a "high number of flood related incidents" for areas up to Stokesley and Hutton Rudby.

Skipton and surrounding villages were also hit by flooding after torrential showers yesterday.

Flash flooding on a number of routes in the area, including the A65, the A59 and the A620, forced some roads to close temporarily but all routes in the Skipton area later reopened, said North Yorkshire Police.

Firefighters had to help a man from his car which was stuck in two feet of water on the A629 at Low Bradley.

Crews also helped to divert water gushing into a garden from a blocked drain in the village.

Yesterday morning a people carrier was found abandoned in water in Carleton.

Lake view: A train makes its way alongside flood water on the outskirts of Skipton.
Picture: Gerard Binks.

Two injured by lightning strike

TWO teenagers were taken to hospital yesterday after being struck by lightning.

The girls, aged 13 and 15, suffered serious but non life-threatening burns in the incident at Ipswich High School, in nearby Woolverstone, at about 4pm.

The girls, who remained conscious throughout, were being treated in hospital.

Rush-hour commuters made their way home through hail storms. Thunderstorms brought torrential downpours to southern counties of England.

July 3: Resident Carl Harris of Toll Bar, near Doncaster, went home for the first time since the floods nine days earlier, and found it still under water.